Nonfiction for Elementary School

A Sentence-Composing Approach

A Student Worktext

Don and Jenny Killgallon

HEINEMANN
Portsmouth, NH

Heinemann
361 Hanover Street
Portsmouth, NH 03801–3912
www.heinemann.com

Offices and agents throughout the world

Cataloging-in-Publication Data is on file at the Library of Congress.

ISBN: 978-0-325-08112-0

Editor: Tobey Antao
Production: Victoria Merecki
Cover and interior designs: Monica Ann Crigler
Typesetter: Cape Cod Compositors, Inc.
Manufacturing: Steve Bernier

Printed in the United States of America on acid-free paper

21 20 19 18 17 EBM 1 2 3 4 5

CONTENTS

NONFICTION: WORDS, SENTENCES, PARAGRAPHS

Throughout this worktext you will learn the meanings of words in featured nonfiction selections, read tidbits of interesting nonfiction, and learn how their authors build sentences and paragraphs in ways you can use in your own writing.

QUICKSHOTS: A WORD ABOUT WORDS   1

   Your Turn: **Understanding Quickshots   2**

NONFICTION: WORDS FROM REAL LIFE   4

BUILDING BETTER SENTENCES

Sentences are built from three different parts: subject, predicate, and tool. Although every sentence needs a subject and a predicate, you'll learn that the most important parts of well-built sentences are the sentence-composing tools good writers use. In this book, you'll practice doing what authors do by adding to your sentences powerful tools like theirs.

SUBJECTS AND PREDICATES   9

   Your Turn: **Matching Subjects and Predicates   11**

SENTENCE-COMPOSING TOOLS   12

   Your Turn: **Identifying Sentence Parts   20**

FRAGMENTS   24

   Your Turn: **Repairing Broken Sentences   29**

UNSCRAMBLING NONFICTION SENTENCES   31

Your Turn: Arranging Sentence-Composing Tools   37

IMITATING NONFICTION SENTENCES   39

Your Turn: Imitating a Model Paragraph   51

A   N O N F I C T I O N   S A M P L E R

A sampler is a collection of short examples. In this sampler, featuring interesting nonfiction tidbits, you'll strengthen your ability to read nonfiction and put your new sentence-composing tools to work to build strong sentences and paragraphs.

INFORMATIONAL TEXT TIDBITS

NEAT INVENTIONS   55

CARS: FROM HORSE DRIVEN TO COMPUTER DRIVEN   56

Your Turn: Nonfiction Sentences About Cars   64

MUSIC: FROM PREHISTORIC TO ELECTRONIC   65

Your Turn: Nonfiction Sentences About Music   73

PLUMBING: FROM OUTSIDE TO INSIDE   74

Your Turn: Nonfiction Sentences About Plumbing   81

COMPUTERS: FROM GIGANTIC TO MICROSCOPIC   83

Your Turn: Nonfiction Sentences About Computers   91

FUN INVENTIONS: AN ASSORTMENT OF ENJOYMENT   92

Your Turn: Mini Research Report   94

ESSAY TIDBITS

QUOTABLE QUOTES 98

Your Turn: Memoir 112

BIOGRAPHICAL TIDBITS

POPULAR AUTHORS 116

J. K. ROWLING: WILD ABOUT HARRY 117

Your Turn: Nonfiction Paragraph Imitation 121

A. A. MILNE: CHRISTOPHER ROBIN AND FRIENDS 123

Your Turn: Nonfiction Paragraph Imitation 127

E. B. WHITE: A BELOVED PIG AND SPIDER 129

Your Turn: Nonfiction Paragraph Imitation 133

J. R. R. TOLKIEN: LORD OF THE FANTASIES 135

Your Turn: Nonfiction Paragraph Imitation 139

DR. SEUSS: SILLY BUT GREAT RHYMES AND DRAWINGS 141

Your Turn: Nonfiction Paragraph Imitation 145

THE BIG DEAL: WRITING A BIOGRAPHICAL ESSAY 147

WORDS OF WIT AND WISDOM 151

Nothing is more satisfying than to write a good sentence.

—Barbara Tuchman, two-time winner of the Pulitzer Prize for nonfiction

----

QUICKSHOTS: A WORD ABOUT WORDS

Nonfiction writing is made up of paragraphs. Paragraphs are made up of sentences. Sentences are made up of words. Sentences and the words they contain—the building blocks of meaning in nonfiction—are sometimes hard to understand, often because of unfamiliar words.

Some words in this worktext may be new to you. Don't worry. For those words, you'll see a quickshot definition **adjacent to** [*beside*] the new word, which is bolded. (You just saw your first quickshot.)

Take this sentence by Rudolph Giuliani, then mayor of New York City, addressing the General Assembly of the United Nations on October 1, 2001, condemning the tragedy of terrorist attacks on September 11, 2001.

*There's no moral way to sympathize
with grossly immoral actions.*

Perhaps a problem is the word *moral* and its opposite *immoral*. The meaning of the sentence is roughly this: *There's no [SOMETHING] way to sympathize with grossly [SOMETHING] actions.* What way? What actions?

So what can you do? Perhaps take time out for dictionary diving to find out what *moral* means (and its opposite *immoral*).

But, to save you time and trouble, in this worktext there's a quicker, easier way called "quickshots."

Throughout this worktext when individual words are **bold**, a fast definition—a quickshot—will be adjacent in brackets. If you already know the word, just skip ahead. If you don't know the word or aren't sure, the quickshot will get you through the sentence without stumbling.

Though not a thorough definition, a quickshot will at least help you to keep reading. As a result, you can avoid a deep dictionary dive and keep reading, stumble-free. Now here is Mayor Giuliani's comment with quickshots.

> *There's no **moral** [right] way to sympathize*
> *with grossly **immoral** [wrong] actions.*

Now you get the mayor's message: there's no right way to approve wrong actions.

Quickshots are a short but not perfect definition. For example, you now know that *moral* means right, *immoral* means wrong. But know also that *moral* and *immoral* refer only to human behavior being right or wrong. If you got most of the words right on a spelling test, you wouldn't say, "I got most spellings moral, but some immoral."

YOUR TURN: UNDERSTANDING QUICKSHOTS

Give quickshots a try with a nonfiction paragraph from a true story about airmen whose plane was shot down over the ocean. They are struggling to survive, despite unbearable heat, little food or water, and the constant threat of sharks circling their raft.

You'll see the paragraph twice: first without quickshots, and then with quickshots. Probably you'll find the second one much easier with quickshot help for some of the words.

Paragraph without Quickshots

(1) On that morning of the twenty-seventh day, the men heard a distant, deep **strumming**. (2) Every airman knew that sound: **pistons**. (3) Their eyes caught a **glint** in the sky—a plane, high overhead. (4) Zamperini fired two **flares** and shook powdered dye into the water, **enveloping** the rafts in a circle of **vivid** orange. (5) The plane kept going, slowly disappearing. (6) The men **sagged**. (7) Then the sound returned, and the plane came back into view. (8) The crew had seen them. (9) With arms shrunken to little more than bone and yellowed skin, the **castaways** waved and shouted, their voices thin from thirst. (10) The plane dropped low and swept alongside the rafts. (11) Zamperini saw the **profiles** of the crewmen, dark against bright

blueness. (12) There was a terrific roaring sound. (13) The water, and the rafts themselves, seemed to boil. (14) It was machine gun fire. (15) This was not an American rescue plane. (16) It was a Japanese bomber. (17) The men **pitched** themselves into the water and hung together under the rafts, **cringing** as bullets punched through the rubber and sliced **effervescent** lines in the water around their faces.

—Laura Hillenbrand, *Unbroken*

Paragraph with Quickshots

(1) On that morning of the twenty-seventh day, the men heard a distant, deep **strumming** [*noise*]. (2) Every airman knew that sound: **pistons** [*engines*]. (3) Their eyes caught a **glint** [*flash*] in the sky—a plane, high overhead. (4) Zamperini fired two **flares** [*bright lights*] and shook powdered dye into the water, **enveloping** [*enclosing*] the rafts in a circle of **vivid** [*bright*] orange. (5) The plane kept going, slowly disappearing. (6) The men **sagged** [*slumped*]. (7) Then the sound returned, and the plane came back into view. (8) The crew had seen them. (9) With arms shrunken to little more than bone and yellowed skin, the **castaways** [*stranded men*] waved and shouted, their voices thin from thirst. (10) The plane dropped low and swept alongside the rafts. (11) Zamperini saw the **profiles** [*faces*] of the crewmen, dark against bright blueness. (12) There was a terrific roaring sound. (13) The water, and the rafts themselves, seemed to boil. (14) It was machine gun fire. (15) This was not an American rescue plane. (16) It was a Japanese bomber. (17) The men **pitched** [*threw*] themselves into the water and hung together under the rafts, **cringing** [*shaking*] as bullets punched through the rubber and sliced **effervescent** [*bubbly*] lines in the water around their faces.

The paragraph above, about the airmen on rafts in the ocean, is from a true story. It really happened. It is an example of nonfiction.

NONFICTION: WORDS FROM REAL LIFE

Fiction is any story, short or long (novel), realistic or fantastic, written mostly from the author's imagination. A fictional story never really happened except in the author's imagination. Think Harry Potter.

A nonfictional story did really happen and is based upon fact. Think Harry Truman, American two-term president from 1945 to 1953, whose biography *Truman* by David McCollough is a nonfiction account of Harry Truman's life.

Another difference is that nonfiction is based upon the real world. Fiction is based upon an imaginary world. Harry Potter, in actuality, couldn't fly on a broomstick during Quidditch. However, in the make-believe of fiction, through the skill and creativity of author J. K. Rowling (and through CGI in the movie versions), Harry appears to be actually flying during Quidditch matches in the wizardly world at Hogwarts. Because of Rowling's skill in creating its realistic details, the flying seems to be actual—but isn't.

In actuality, though, President Harry Truman did order the first and only military use of an atomic bomb to speed the end of World War II. The bombing actually happened on August 6 in the city of Hiroshima, Japan, and August 9, 1945, in Nagasaki, Japan. The true story of one of those two cities is a nonfiction book titled *Hiroshima* by John Hersey.

The main difference between fiction and nonfiction is that fiction reflects scenes from an author's imagination, and nonfiction reflects events from an author's investigation and discovery. Fiction writers imagine, then invent. Nonfiction writers research, then report.

Much nonfiction, like most fiction, tells stories—but real stories of actual events (history or current events), or of real people (biography). Nonfiction authors try to tell those stories truthfully, factually, to reflect accurately the event or the person they write about.

Here is a quick look at the major kinds of nonfiction.

NONFICTION TYPES

1. *History: Description of a past incident or event*

   Excerpt: After the Englishmen landed at Plymouth in 1620, most of them probably would have starved to death but for **aid** [*help*] of friendly natives of the New World.

   —Dee Brown, *Bury My Heart at Wounded Knee:*
   An Indian History of the American West

2. *Journalism: News of a current incident or event*

   Excerpt: In 1932, the *New York Times* had this headline: "Charles Augustus Lindbergh, Jr., 20-month-old son of Colonel and Mrs. Charles A. Lindbergh, was kidnapped from his crib in the **nursery** [*baby's room*] on the second floor of his parents' home."

   —David Randall, *The Great Reporters*

3. *Instruction: Directions for accomplishing a task, a goal, an outcome*

   Excerpt: One **primary** [*important*] purpose in this book is to teach you how to cook so that you will understand the **fundamental techniques** [*basic methods*].

   —Julia Childs, *Mastering the Art of French Cooking*

4. *Essay: Thoughts, opinions, or judgments of a writer*

   Excerpt: If you never let your son climb a tree because he might fall and hurt himself, or if you refuse to let the little league coach make him sit out the big game because he was late to practice, or if you never make your daughter do what is right even though it hurts, you are guaranteeing that they will never grow up, and that they will **remain** [stay] emotional babies all their life.

   —James Robert Ross, *An Opinion on Most Everything*

5. **True Story:** *Real event told as a narrative*

   Excerpt: Six **regiments** [*groups of soldiers*], accompanied by **cavalry** [*horse solders*] that rode in ahead of the **infantry** [*foot soldiers*], pressed on above Alexandria and reached a climax on the night of March 21 with a surprise attack, through rain and hail and darkness, that captured a whole regiment of rebel cavalry caught off guard by the **assault** [*attack*].

   —Shelby Foote, The Civil War: A Narrative (adapted)

6. **Autobiography and Biography:** *Story of someone's life, written by that person (autobiography) or another person (biography)*

   Excerpt: It is with a kind of fear that I begin to write the history of my life. I have, as it were, a superstitious **hesitation** [*reluctance*] in lifting the veil that clings about my childhood like a golden mist. (autobiography)

   —Helen Keller, *The Story of My Life*

   Excerpt: In a sunlit room, Helen Keller sat beside the deathbed of Annie Sullivan, Helen's teacher and lifelong companion. Annie had died minutes before, and Helen was **consumed** [*filled*] with grief. (biography)

   —Dorothy Herrmann, *Helen Keller: A Life* (adapted)

7. **Quotation:** *Short, well-expressed wise idea taken from a longer work—a poem, a book, a speech, a conversation*

   Excerpt: Don't judge each day by the harvest you reap but by the seeds you plant. *(This is a memorable saying by author Robert Louis Stevenson.)*

   —Steven Price, *1001 Smartest Things People Ever Said*

8. **Report:** *Summary of research about a topic*

   Excerpt: People have reported balloons, airplanes, stars, and many other common objects as unidentified flying objects (UFOs). The people who make such reports don't recognize these common objects because something in their surroundings temporarily **assumes** [*takes on*] an unfamiliar appearance.
   —Edward J. Ruppelt, *The Report on Unidentified Flying Objects*

9. **Informational Text:** *Presentation of facts about a topic*

   Excerpt: Baby undershirts come in three kinds: pull-over, side-snap closing, and a one-piece type that slips over the head and snaps to the diaper.
   —Benjamin Spock, *Baby and Child Care*

10. **Review:** *Rating of something—a product, a company, a book, a movie, a TV show, a song, a concert, and so forth*

    Excerpt: The **vast** [*huge*] and free **gourmet** [*superb*] food selection is only one reason *Google* was ranked as the world's best place to work. Employees are treated to massages, haircuts, access to three wellness centers, a bowling alley, basketball courts, a roller-hockey rink, ping-pong tables, arcade games, a rock-climbing wall, and indoor volleyball courts complete with actual sand. Not to be forgotten are the heated toilet seats.
    —Ron Friedman, *The Best Place to Work* (adapted)

In *Nonfiction for Elementary School: A Sentence-Composing Approach*, you'll read nonfiction of various types—usually excerpts of sentences or paragraphs. You'll learn to read nonfiction more deeply, see how nonfiction authors build strong sentences, and learn to build your own sentences like theirs.

NONFICTION TOPICS

What are the topics of nonfiction? Count the number of grains of sand in all the deserts of the earth, and then count the number of drops of water in all the oceans on the planet, and then multiply both figures by a billion trillion. That's how many topics nonfiction has been written about—from A to Z, cars, travel, sports, health, friendship, presidents, money, celebrities, history, mystery, weather, education, and a gazillion more.

In *Nonfiction for Elementary School: A Sentence-Composing Approach*, you'll read just a small sample of nonfiction, but through the activities, you'll increase your ability to read nonfiction more deeply and write nonfiction more skillfully.

Reading is to the mind what exercise is to the body.

—Richard Steele

SUBJECTS AND PREDICATES

A sentence tells people something about a topic. The topic is called *a subject*. The comment about the topic is called *a predicate*. Subjects are topics, and predicates are comments about them. Every sentence needs both a subject and a predicate.

THESE ARE JUST TOPICS, NOT SENTENCES

1. The length of sharks
2. The majority of modern sharks
3. Many sharks
4. Sharks that feed on fish
5. Almost one-third of a shark's body
6. Some shark species, through their keen sense of smell,
7. The average number of deaths resulting from shark attacks each year
8. To avoid a shark attack
9. Only four species out of the total number 470 species of sharks
10. The great white, oceanic white tip, tiger, and bull sharks

THESE ARE JUST COMMENTS, NOT SENTENCES

1. ranges from seven inches to thirty-nine feet
2. trace back one hundred million years
3. lose thousands of teeth during their lifetimes
4. have needle-like teeth
5. is made up of its liver
6. can detect one part per million of blood in ocean water
7. is less than six throughout the world

8. requires not splashing around or wearing shiny objects like jewelry

9. have been involved in fatal attacks on people

10. are those four species

The two lists above are not sentences. They are only topics and comments. A sentence is a group of words with a topic (called "*a subject*") and a comment about that topic (called "*a predicate*"). Following, the ten topics and ten comments about those topics are linked to make ten complete sentences, each with a subject and a predicate—the two sentence parts every sentence needs.

SUBJECT (topic)	PREDICATE (comment about the topic)
1. The length of sharks	ranges from seven inches to thirty-nine feet.
2. The majority of modern sharks	trace back one hundred million years.
3. Many sharks	lose thousands of teeth during their lifetimes.
4. Sharks that feed on fish	have needle-like teeth.
5. Almost one-third of a shark's body	is made up of its liver.
6. Some shark species, through their keen sense of smell,	can detect one part per million of blood in ocean water.
7. The average number of deaths resulting from shark attacks each year	is less than six throughout the world.
8. To avoid a shark attack	requires not splashing around or wearing shiny objects like jewelry.
9. Only four species out of the total number 470 species of sharks	have been involved in fatal attacks on people.
10. The great white, oceanic white tip, tiger, and bull sharks	are those four species.

YOUR TURN: MATCHING SUBJECTS AND PREDICATES

Match the subject with its predicate to make a sentence. Write out each sentence.

SUBJECT	PREDICATE
1. Shakespeare ^ . —Academy of American Poets (Web site), *"Shakespeare"*	**a.** was so tangled in the rope that her small body was curled like a horseshoe, her mouth pulling close to her tail
2. A man named Albert Einstein ^ . —Barack Obama, *"Of Thee I Sing: A Letter to My Daughters"*	**b.** taught me a lot about my mother's family history
3. Living in my grandparents' house ^ . —Rosa Parks, *My Story*	**c.** may weigh more than 400 pounds, about the weight of ten second-grade children
4. The baby dolphin ^ . —Craig and Juliana Hatkoff, *Winter's Tale*	**d.** turned pictures in his mind into giant advances in science, changing the world with energy and light
5. Fully grown male mountain gorillas ^ . —Seymour Simon, *Gorillas*	**e.** wrote more than 30 plays

SENTENCE-COMPOSING TOOLS

What makes the best hamburger? First, you'll need two basics: bread and meat. Then you want more: maybe cheese, catsup or mustard, onions, tomato, lettuce, pickles, and so forth. Add-ons make it tastier, and the best.

What makes the best sentence? First, you'll need two basics: a subject and a predicate. For best sentences, add-ons to a subject and a predicate make your sentences "tastier" for readers. The add-ons are built by sentence-composing tools like ones authors use.

Tools are sentence parts added to a sentence to provide information beyond the subject and predicate. Those tools help you add details and dazzle to your sentences and paragraphs.

ACTIVITY 1: TOOL TALK

The first sentence in each pair has just a subject and predicate, with no tools. The second sentence also has a subject and predicate but includes sentence-composing tools as well. That sentence, the one the author wrote, says more and is more interesting. Tell what extra information the tools provide.

EXAMPLE (*Tools are bolded and have commas that separate them from the rest of the sentence.*)

a. Spectators at the huge fire responded by chopping up wooden fences and sidewalks.

b. Spectators at the huge fire, **who were asked to help**, responded by chopping up wooden fences and sidewalks, **hoping to deprive the fire of fuel**. (*contains two tools*)

　　　　　　　　　　　　　—Jim Murphy, *The Great Fire*

SAMPLE TOOL TALK

The first tool tells readers what the spectators were asked to do (*who were asked to help*). The tool at the end of the sentence tells why the spectators were chopping up things (*hoping to deprive the fire of fuel*).

1a. Jackie Robinson actually preferred football and starred on UCLA's team.

1b. Although he became famous playing baseball, Jackie Robinson actually preferred football and starred on UCLA's team. (*contains one tool*)

—Barry Denenberg, *Stealing Home*

2a. The Atocha is a treasure ship.

2b. The Atocha is a treasure ship, **laden [*filled*] with gold, jewels, silver bars, and thousands of coins.** (*contains one tool*)

—Gail Gibbons, *Sunken Treasure*

3a. Almost anything can set it off without warning.

3b. When black powder is too dry or mixed in the wrong formula, almost anything can set it off without warning. (*contains one tool*)

—John Fleischman, *Phineas Gage*

4a. Most immigrants came from England, Holland, and France.

4b. When the thirteen colonies were first settled, most immigrants came from England, Holland, and France, **followed soon afterwards by Scandinavians, Welsh, Scots, Scot-Irish, Irish, and Germans.** (*contains two tools*)

—Ellen Levine, *If Your Name Was Changed at Ellis Island*

5a. Leo was rescued by a kind goatherd and his family.

5b. Luckily, Leo, **the snow leopard cub,** was rescued by a kind goatherd and his family, **who hand-fed Leo and kept him safe.** (*contains three tools*)

—Craig and Isabella Hatkoff, *Leo the Snow Leopard*

6a. A truly great quarterback plays at a very high level on the field and off the field as well.

6b. In my opinion, a truly great quarterback plays at a very high level on the field—and off the field as well, **a guy who plays like a champion, not only on Sundays but also on every other day of the week.** *(contains three tools)*

—Mark Brunell and Drew Brees, *Coming Back Stronger*

7a. Crowds lined the parade route.

7b. Crowds lined the parade route, **hoping to get a glimpse of Archduke Franz Ferdinand, heir to the imperial throne of Austria-Hungary, seat of the thousand-year-old Hapsburg Empire.** *(contains three tools)*

—Russell Freedman, *The War to End All Wars*

8a. Anne was living with her father and mother and her sister Margot in a housing development in Amsterdam.

8b. During the war in 1942, Anne was living with her father and mother and her sister Margot, **who was three years older than Anne**, in a housing development in Amsterdam, **the capital city of the Netherlands.** *(contains three tools)*

—Ruud Van Der Roi, *Anne Frank*

9a. I dreamed that I was shot in my side.

9b. That night, when I finally managed to drift off to sleep, I dreamed that I was shot in my side, **with people running past me without helping, as they were all running for their lives.** *(contains four tools)*

—Ishmael Beah, *A Long Way Gone*

10a. Abraham Woodhull visited New York markets and coffeehouses.

10b. During the American Revolution, spying for the Patriots, Abraham Woodhull, **a slight man who rarely spoke above a whisper,** visited New York markets and coffeehouses, **keeping his eyes and ears open for any useful information about the plans of the British Army.** (contains four tools)

—Paul Janeczko, *The Dark Game*

Question: What two sentence parts cannot be removed without destroying the sentence? What sentence parts can be removed?

Answer: The subject and the predicate cannot be removed. Take out either, and the sentence is destroyed. Tools can be removed, but nobody wants to remove them because they're often the best parts of the sentence, adding detail and dazzle!

Look back at the ten sentences with tools. Which have tools at the beginning of the sentence? Which have tools in the middle? Which have tools at the end? Which have tools in more than one place? All those places are ones where tools can be added to build a stronger sentence.

SUMMARY

Every sentence must have at least one subject and at least one predicate. Most sentences also have sentence-composing tools to make them stronger. Example sentences on the following pages are adapted from the nonfiction book *Fast Food Nation* by Eric Schlosser, selected by *Time* magazine as one of the hundred best nonfiction books.

SUBJECT FACTS

A subject is the topic of a sentence. It tells what the sentence is about.

1. Subjects can be at the very beginning of the sentence.	**The pizza deliveryman** drops off his pizza and collects his tip.
2. Subjects can even be at the end of a sentence.	Up the road winds **the pizza delivery-man**.
3. Subjects can be short.	**McDonald's** has about twenty-eight thousand restaurants worldwide.
4. Subjects can be long.	**An industry that began with a handful of modest hot dog and hamburger stands in southern California** has spread to every corner of the nation.
5. Subjects can do just one thing.	**People** rarely consider where fast food comes from.
6. Subjects can do more than one thing.	**People** just grab their tray off the counter, find a table, take a seat, unwrap the paper, and dig in.
7. Sentences can have just one subject.	**Customers** should know what really lurks between those sesame seed buns.
8. Sentences can have more than one subject.	**Subdivisions, shopping malls, and fast food restaurants** are appearing everywhere.
9. Sentences without a subject won't make sense.	**???** never appears on the menu. *(no subject)* *Without a subject, we don't know what never appears on the menu.*

PREDICATE FACTS

A predicate is a comment about the subject (topic) of a sentence.

1. Predicates usually come after the subject.	McDonald's **annually hires about one million people.**
2. Predicates sometimes come before the subject.	**Employed by McDonald's has been** one out of every eight workers in the United States.
3. Predicates can be short.	McDonald's **operates playgrounds.**
4. Predicates can be long.	Fast food **happens at restaurants and drive-throughs, at stadiums, airports, zoos, elementary and middle and high schools, universities, on cruise ships, trains, and airplanes.**
5. Predicates can tell just one thing.	Fast food **infiltrated every nook and cranny of American society.**
6. Predicates can tell more than one thing.	McDonald's **has about twenty-eight thousand restaurants worldwide** and **opens almost two thousand more every year.**
7. Sentences without predicates won't make sense.	Buying fast food **???** (*no predicate*) *Without a predicate, we don't know what happens when buying fast food.*

SENTENCE-COMPOSING TOOL FACTS

A tool is a sentence part that adds detail and dazzle to a sentence.

1. Tools can be placed at the *beginning*, *middle*, or *end* of a sentence.	OPENER (appears at the beginning, with a *comma after the tool*) **In 2015**, Americans spent more than $150 billion on fast food. S-V SPLIT (appears between a subject and verb with a *comma before and after the tool*) The fast food industry, **during a short period of time**, has transformed our landscape, economy, workforce, and popular culture. CLOSER (appears at the end with a *comma before the tool*) Half of the money spent on food is spent at restaurants, **mainly fast food restaurants**.
2. A tool can be a word.	WORD **Indeed**, McDonald's earns its profits mainly from collecting rents.
3. A tool can be a *phrase*. A phrase is a group of words without a subject and predicate.	PHRASE **Adjusted for inflation**, the hourly wage of the average U. S. worker peaked in 1973 and then steadily declined for the next twenty-five years.
4. A tool can be a *dependent clause*. A dependent clause is a sentence part with a subject and predicate. It is not a sentence, but a part of a sentence.	DEPENDENT CLAUSE **When employees get tired of cafeteria food**, they often send somebody out for takeout food.

5. Sentences can have many tools, together or apart.	MANY TOOLS TOGETHER The thinking behind fast food has become the system of today's economy, **wiping out small businesses, obliterating regional differences, spreading identical stores throughout the country.** *(three phrases in a row)* MANY TOOLS APART **While a handful of fast food workers rise up the corporate ladder,** the majority lack full-time employment, **quitting after only a few months.** *(dependent clause/phrase)*
6. Tools can be short, medium, or long.	SHORT *(1–5 words)* Buying fast food has become so routine that it is taken for granted, **like brushing your teeth.** MEDIUM *(6–10 words)* Fast food ads, **full of thick juicy burgers and long golden fries,** rarely mention where these foods come from or what they contain. LONG *(10+ words)* **During the economic boom of the 1990s when many American workers enjoyed their first pay wages in a generation,** the real value of wages in the restaurant industry continued to fall.

YOUR TURN: IDENTIFYING SENTENCE PARTS

In each sentence, one part is the subject, and one is the predicate. The other parts are tools adding more details. In the lists, tell the kind of sentence part: *subject*, *predicate*, or *tool*.

Remember: A *subject* is a topic. A *predicate* is a comment about the topic. A *tool* is a sentence part telling more information.

EXAMPLE

> **a.** Working slowly, *(tool)*
>
> **b.** deliberately, *(tool)*
>
> **c.** Louis Braille *(subject)*
>
> **d.** punched tiny holes across the page with the sharp point of a stylus. *(predicate)*
> > —Russell Freedman, *Out of Darkness*

1a. Blanketed [*covered*] with a soft coat of snow or hot to the touch from the rays of the sun,

1b. the statue

1c. gives off a great feeling of power, accomplishment, and strength.
> —Elizabeth Cody Kimmel, *Balto and the Great Race*

2a. The iceberg,

2b. wet and glistening,

2c. towered far above the **forecastle** [*forward*] deck of the *Titanic*.
> —Walter Lord, *A Night to Remember*

3a. While she sat there,

3b. a fuzzy spider

3c. paced across the room.

—Eleanor Coerr, *Sadako and the Thousand Paper Cranes*

4a. In Alaska outside the big towns and cities,

4b. houses

4c. may be hundreds of miles away from each other.

—Elizabeth Cody Kimmel, *Balto and the Great Race*

5a. The Anderson kid

5b. got the nickname Einstein after Albert Einstein,

5c. a brilliant thinker and the most famous scientist of the twentieth century.

—Seymour Simon, *Einstein Anderson*

6a. Although he was a strict **taskmaster** [*boss*] within his home,

6b. Dad

6c. **tolerated** [*allowed*] no criticism of the family from outsiders.

—Frank B. Gilbreth, *Cheaper by the Dozen*

7a. Lost in his studies,

7b. Oppenheimer

7c. paid little attention to the outside world.

—Steve Sheinkin, *Bomb*

8a. The owner of the *Titanic*,

8b. a company called the White Star Line,

8c. spared no expense in making this the best ship afloat.

—Thomas Conklin, *The Titanic Sinks!*

9a. Tornadoes

9b. travel more than two hundred miles along the ground,

9c. leaving enormous damage in their **wake** [*path*].

—Seymour Simon, *Tornadoes*

10a. The Declaration of Independence,

10b. which was signed by members of the Continental Congress July 4, 1776,

10c. showed that the colonies wanted to be free.

—Kay Moore, *If You Lived at the Time of the American Revolution*

Note: *Sentences 11–15 have two or more tools.*

11a. While everyone scattered,

11b. I

11c. crept into my favorite hiding place,

11d. the little closet tucked under the stairs.

—Jean Fritz, *Homesick: My Own Story*

12a. In plain sight now,

12b. within our den,

12c. we

12d. found four baby raccoons a month old perhaps.

—Sterling North, *Rascal*

13a. On January 28, 1986,

13b. *Challenger,*

13c. a spacecraft designed to **transport** [*carry*], protect, and nurture its seven-member crew as it transported them,

13d. was engulfed in a fiery **inferno** [*huge blaze*] in full view of thousands of people at the space center and millions of others viewing the launch on television.

—Hugh Harris, Challenger: An American Tragedy

14a. Still in pajamas,

14b. Harry Gold

14c. raced around his cluttered bedroom,

14d. pulling out desk drawers,

14e. tossing boxes out of the closet,

14f. and yanking books from the shelves.

—Steve Sheinkin, Bomb

15a. As a volunteer emergency ambulance driver,

15b. when I was called to car accidents and saw people I knew were dead,

15c. I

15d. would keep working on them,

15e. because I could not bring myself to accept their deaths.

—Gary Paulsen, Guts

FRAGMENTS

Did you ever accidentally drop a glass plate and it hit the floor and shattered into fragments? The plate, broken, was useless. Sometimes, accidentally, writers break sentences, too. Those sentences, fragmented, are broken so badly that readers have a hard time gluing their meaning back together.

But there's hope. Even plates broken into fragments can sometimes be repaired. Broken sentences can be, too. In this section, you won't learn how to repair broken plates, but you will learn how to fix broken sentences.

TOO LITTLE SENTENCE: FRAGMENTS

A fragment is "too little" sentence—a sentence part mistakenly written like a whole sentence—with a capital letter at the beginning and a period at the end. Because readers expect a whole sentence when they see something that begins with a capital letter and ends with a period, fragments confuse readers: a fragment is a broken sentence that should be a part of a whole sentence. Readers expect *whole* sentences, not broken sentences.

ACTIVITY 1: FINDING BROKEN SENTENCES

In each list, identify four broken sentences (fragments) and one whole sentence. The fragments masquerade as sentences—starting with a capital letter and ending with a period—but are actually just parts of a sentence. A whole sentence needs a subject and a predicate. If either is missing, it's broken.

LIST ONE

1. Once set in motion.

2. Unlike most other large animals.

3. To hoe the weeds, to dig our careful rows, and then to push the seeds gently into the soft soil.

4. Running more than 2,100 miles along America's Eastern Seaboard, through the serene and beckoning Appalachian Mountains.

5. Fleet and Lee stood quietly side by side, watching the ice draw nearer.

LIST TWO

6. And taking care of other people's children.

7. He reached the fruit and dropped it to the third boy, who stood below, holding out his coat as a blanket.

8. And never bothered coming back.

9. Although some Dutch women in 1937 were wearing their skirts knee-length.

10. Involving 164 ships, 3,000 landing craft, and some 280,000 American troops.

Only two (#5, #7) are sentences because only they contain a topic (subject) and a comment about the topic (predicate)—the two requirements for every sentence. The rest are fragments because they are sentence parts, not whole sentences. Because they start with a capital letter and end with a period, they start and end like sentences, but aren't.

Here are the original sentences. The broken sentences have been repaired by gluing them as a part of a whole sentence.

1. Once set in motion, each country's army moved with surprising speed.

   —Jim Murphy, *Truce*

2. Unlike most other large animals, sharks don't have bones or a hard skeleton.

   —Steve Jenkins, *Bones*

3. Every planting season, my sister and I would wake up before dawn to hoe the weeds, to dig our careful rows, and then to push the seeds gently into the soft soil.

—William Kamkwamba and Bryan Mealer,
The Boy Who Harnessed the Wind

4. Running more than 2,100 miles along America's Eastern Seaboard, through the serene and beckoning Appalachian Mountains, the Appalachian Trail is the granddaddy of long hikes.

—Bill Bryson, *A Walk in the Woods*

5. **[THE ONLY SENTENCE FROM LIST ONE]** Fleet and Lee stood quietly side by side, watching the ice draw nearer.

—Walter Lord, *A Night to Remember*

6. Mrs. Carson had no job skills or work experience so the only way she could support herself and her two sons was by cleaning houses and taking care of other people's children.

—Ben Carson, *Gifted Hands*

7. **[THE ONLY SENTENCE FROM LIST TWO]** He reached the fruit and dropped it to the third boy, who stood below holding out his coat as a blanket.

—Christy Brown, *My Left Foot*

8. The other businesses looked like someone left for lunch decades earlier and never bothered coming back.

—Rebecca Skloot, *The Immortal Life of Henrietta Lacks*

9. Although some Dutch women in 1937 were wearing their skirts knee-length, mine were still a cautious three inches above my shoes.

   —Corrie ten Boom, *The Hiding Place*

10. The invasion at Lingayen Gulf on the morning of January 9, 1945 was one of the most **monumental** [*huge*] operations of World War II, involving 164 ships, 3,000 landing craft, and some 280,000 American troops.

    —Hampton Sides, *Ghost Soldiers*

ACTIVITY 2: REPAIRING BROKEN SENTENCES

Repair the broken sentences (fragments) by gluing them at the caret (^) into the sentence where they belong from the list on the left.

Sentences	Broken Sentences
1. Flames from the burning hay in the barn's **loft** [upper space] pushed against the barn's roof and beams, ^ . —Jim Murphy, *The Great Fire*	**a.** like a plane ticket stub, a secret report, a letter from a fellow spy
2. ^ , Hitler wore his dark brown hair parted on the right and kept his mustache carefully combed and trimmed. —Bill O'Reilly, *Hitler's Last Days*	**b.** drinking soda and watching a turtle
3. One early afternoon I looked up from where I sat on the boat dock, ^ . —Dwight Abbot, Danny Abbot, *I Cried, You Didn't Listen*	**c.** almost as if they were struggling to break free
4. Everywhere he looked were incriminating papers, ^ . —Steve Sheinkin, *Bomb*	**d.** leaving the short grass looking wet and weary
5. The frozen earth thawed, ^ . —Peter Abrahams, *Tell Freedom*	**e.** a **fussy** [*picky*] man of **modest** [*small*] height and weight who had frequent emotional outbursts

ACTIVITY 3: DETECTING BROKEN SENTENCES

Read the paragraph to get an idea of the content. Because it has six broken sentences, reading will be bumpy. Glue each broken sentence (fragment) to the sentence where it belongs. Then write out the paragraph. After fixing the broken sentences by eliminating the fragments, you will have a paragraph with exactly six whole sentences and no fragments. Reading will then be smooth, not bumpy.

(1) The United States went through **monumental** [*huge*] changes. (2) Between 1850 and 1900. (3) The Civil War was fought. (4) Putting an end to slavery and **forging** [*joining*] the independent-minded states into a powerful union. (5) Settlers pushed westward. (6) A **transcontinental** [*coast-to-coast*] railroad was built. (7) To **link** [*connect*] the East to the West Coast. (8) Opening the door to **swifter** [*faster*] travel. (9) A great **surge** [*rise*] of immigrants left their homelands overseas. (10) To start a new life in America. (11) In fact, the second half of the nineteenth century saw over sixteen and a half million people settle in the United States. (12) Making this one of the largest voluntary **emigrations** [*moves*] in the history of the world.

—Jim Murphy, *Across America on an Emigrant Train*

ACTIVITY 4: SOLVING A FRAGMENT JIGSAW PUZZLE

This paragraph, about a series of firsts in American transportation in 1903, has to be put back together. Underneath the paragraph are broken sentences (fragments) that should be sentence parts of sentences in the paragraph. Glue each broken sentence to the sentence where it belongs.

On the Mark: At connections with pauses, commas are needed.

"Transportation Firsts in 1903"

(1) It was an age that **spawned** [*produced*] bold dreams and **audacious** [*daring*] dreamers. (2) In 1903 a pair of tinkerers, Wilbur

and Orville Wright, climbed aboard a device of their own invention near Kitty Hawk, North Carolina. (3) In the same year, a Californian named George Adams Wyman rode into New York City aboard a motorcycle. (4) He was the first person to cross the continent on a motorized vehicle, and he had done it in only fifty days. (5) Twenty days later, Horatio Nelson Jackson and his bulldog, Bud, arrived from San Francisco in their **battered** [*shabby*] and muddy **Winton** [*old car*]. (6) In Milwaukee twenty-one-year-old Bill Harley and twenty-year-old Arthur Davidson attached an engine of their own **design** [*invention*] to a **modified** [*altered*] bicycle, hung a sign on the front of their workshop. (7) On July 23 of that same year, Henry Ford sold Dr. Ernst Pfenning a shiny red Model A.

—Daniel James Brown, *The Boys in the Boat*

FRAGMENTS

a. and flew ten feet above the sand for twelve full seconds

b. that had carried him all the way from San Francisco

c. becoming the first to accomplish the feat in an automobile

d. and went into business selling production motorcycles

e. the first of 1,750 that he would sell in the next year and a half

YOUR TURN: REPAIRING BROKEN SENTENCES

Fix each broken sentence by gluing it to the sentence in which it belongs. When you make all repairs, you will have a paragraph of exactly six whole sentences and no broken ones.

(1) There are a number of qualities a lead dog must have. (2) To guide a sled and a team of dogs. (3) The lead dog must know how to respond to the **musher's** [*sled-driver's*] commands. (4) And keep the dog team moving. (5) He must be able to lead the team between trees

and rocks. (6) Without pulling the sled into them. (7) He must be able to avoid sudden obstacles in the snow trail. (8) That the musher on the back of the sled cannot see. (9) He must be able to assert himself over the other dogs on the team. (10) So that he is followed without question. (11) Most important of all. (12) A lead dog must have intuition. (13) Which is a natural inner knowledge of what to do.

—Elizabeth Cody Kimmel, *Balto and the Great Race*

UNSCRAMBLING NONFICTION SENTENCES

Unless they're eggs, things scrambled—like clothes in a drawer or closet, toys scattered on the floor, tools and toys strewn across the basement, or old stuff stored in an attic—are a mess. They drive people crazy because people want order in their lives, not jumbled messes. Getting order and neatness takes work, though. You probably remember times you were told to straighten your room, and, looking around at the mess everywhere, didn't know where to start.

Getting order and neatness in sentences and paragraphs also takes work. Readers want your sentences and paragraphs to be orderly and neat, with your paragraph's sentence parts and sentences in proper places, not in jumbled messes.

In the following activities, you will play with intentionally scrambled sentence parts and scrambled sentences to arrange them into sentences that are orderly and neat. Doing these activities strengthens your reading skill because you have to read each scrambled part carefully to see how it fits into the complete sentence, like looking carefully at a piece of a jigsaw puzzle to decide where it fits in the big picture.

EXAMPLE

The sentence describes a polar bear eating a seal.

SCRAMBLED SENTENCE PARTS

a. turning back the skin and blubber

b. and ate greedily of the hot crimson meat

c. the polar bear ripped up the seal's body

d. letting out a cloud of steam

UNSCRAMBLED SENTENCES
(Two make sense. One doesn't make sense.)

1. The polar bear ripped up the seal's body, turning back the skin and blubber, letting out a cloud of steam, and ate greedily of the hot crimson meat.

2. And ate greedily of the hot crimson meat, turning back the skin and blubber, the polar bear ripped up the seal's body, letting out a cloud of steam.

3. The polar bear ripped up the seal's body, letting out a cloud of steam, turning back the skin and blubber, and ate greedily of the hot crimson meat.

Two of these make sense. The first version is the one Norah Burke wrote in "Polar Night." The third version is also unscrambled well. The second version, though, doesn't make much sense because the bear cannot eat the meat of the seal before removing the skin that covers the seal's flesh.

ACTIVITY 1: UNSCRAMBLING SENTENCE PARTS

Unscramble the sentence parts to create a sentence that makes sense.

On the Mark: Use commas for tools.

1a. and attending Bronx High School of Science

1b. he

1c. skipping grades

1d. was a star student

—Adam Braun, *The Promise of a Pencil*

2a. looked at the snow

2b. that spread to the **horizon** [*skyline*]

2c. and ice

2d. from the deck

2e. Sir Ernest Shackleton

> —Michael McCurdy, *Trapped by the Ice*

3a. was an air-raid siren

3b. the source of the loud frightful wail

3c. hardly a stone's throw from our house

3d. propped on the roof of the brewery

> —Jerry Spinelli, *Knots in My Yo-Yo String*

4a. more than one hundred years ago

4b. breaking his left arm below the elbow

4c. he was up on the roof of the family house replacing some loose tiles

4d. when my father was fourteen

4e. when he slipped and fell

> —Roald Dahl, *Boy*

5a. a health **resort** [*hotel*]

5b. James came home no better

5c. whose mineral waters were supposed to cure all kinds of illnesses

5d. James Madison's father sent him to Warm Springs

5e. but even after drinking gallons of water

> —Jean Fritz, *The Great Little Madison*

6a. guarding our house

6b. was an **exceptionally** [*very*] intelligent and **responsible** [*trustworthy*] Saint Bernard watchdog

6c. Wowser

6d. and lawns and gardens and all my pets

6e. weighing one hundred and seventy pounds

—Sterling North, *Rascal*

7a. because the new practice of reading

7b. that they were farsighted

7c. made Europeans across the continent suddenly realize

7d. Gutenberg's printing press

7e. created a **surge** [*rise*] in demand for **spectacles** [*eyeglasses*]

—Steven Johnson, *How We Got to Now*

8a. I was just kind of rolling along with the waves

8b. and my left arm dangling in the cool water

8c. relaxing on my surfboard

8d. with my right hand on the nose of my board

8e. when suddenly there was a flash of gray

—Bethany Hamilton, *Soul Surfer*

9a. a young man

9b. of "Maria" from *West Side Story*

9c. on a bus trip to London from Oxford University

9d. obviously fresh from a **pub** [*bar*]

9e. breaking into his Irish tenor's **rendition** [*version*]

9f. spotted me and went down on his knees in the aisle

　　　　—Judith Ortiz Cofer, "The Myth of the Latin Woman"

10a. celebrated the end of the Civil War

10b. glowing from candles, torches, gaslights, and fireworks

10c. with a grand **illumination** [*lighting*] of the city

10d. the city of Washington

10e. giving the city the most beautiful night in the history of the capital

10f. on the evening of April 13, 1865

10g. public buildings and private homes

　　　　—James L. Swanson, *Chasing Lincoln's Killer*

ACTIVITY 2: PUTTING SENTENCE PARTS IN GOOD PLACES

Sometimes sentence parts are movable within a sentence. Move the underlined sentence parts to one other good place.

On the Mark: Use commas for tools.

EXAMPLE

Original Place: One of nineteen immigration stations operating around the United States in the early twentieth century, the Angel Island Immigration Station was the main Pacific gateway into and out of the country.

　　　　—Erika Lee and Judy Yung, *Angel Island*

NEW ACCEPTABLE PLACES

1. The Angel Island Immigration Station, <u>one of nineteen immigration stations operating around the United States in the early twentieth century,</u> was the main Pacific gateway into and out of the country.

2. The Angel Island Immigration Station was the main Pacific gateway into and out of the country, <u>one of nineteen immigration stations operating around the United States in the early twentieth century.</u>

---

1. <u>Weighing a mere four ounces,</u> Moonbird has flown more than 325,000 miles in his life, which is the distance to the moon and nearly halfway back.

   —Phillip M. Hoose, *Moonbird*

2. In 1793 in Philadelphia, <u>down on the docks lining the Delaware River,</u> cargo was being loaded onto ships that would sail to New York, Boston, and other distant ports.

   —Jim Murphy, *An American Plague*

3. <u>A six-foot-three, 225-pound Texan,</u> Miller was the ship's heavyweight boxing champ.

   —Steve Sheinkin, *The Port Chicago 50*

4. <u>When he was very young,</u> George Washington Carver kept a garden where he spent hours each day caring for his plants.

   —Aliki Brandenberg, *A Weed Is a Flower*

5. <u>Long before people came to Puerto Rico,</u> hundreds of thousands of parrots flew over the island and smaller islands nearby.

   —Susan L. Roth and Cindy Trumbore, *Parrots over Puerto Rico*

6. The great mansion, which stretched for three miles along the now-frozen river, blazed with light, <u>its massive crystal and gold chandeliers reflecting a hundred times in the mirrored walls of its cathedral-size reception rooms.</u>

   —Candace Fleming, *The Family Romanov*

7. Heads now **aligned** [*close*] <u>with only inches apart,</u> the two elephants locked eyes and squared up again.

   —Caitlin O'Connell, *Elephant Don*

8. I picture myself sitting at the bottom of the stairs, <u>shaking with fear, frightened of every sound I may hear from above.</u>

   —Dave Pelzer, *The Lost Boy*

9. Ethel had grown up an orphan in Tacoma, Washington, <u>living with an older sister after her parents died.</u>

   —Mary Cronk Farrell, *Pure Grit*

10. <u>Impossibly soft, with a rounded face, button eyes, pink nose, upright ears and a long thick tail,</u> the tree kangaroo was about the size of a small dog or an overweight cat.

    —Sy Montgomery, *The Quest for the Tree Kangaroo*

YOUR TURN: ARRANGING SENTENCE-COMPOSING TOOLS

During the Second World War, an American bomber and its crew were shot down and landed in the ocean. The surviving crew, with almost no provisions of food or clothes, drifted twenty-seven days over 1,000 miles in shark-infested water. The true story of the crew's plight is memorably told in *Unbroken: A World War II Story of Survival, Resilience, and Redemption*, by Laura Hillenbrand.

Directions: The following activity is based upon the first paragraph of that true story. From the stripped-down paragraph that follows, sentence-composing tools have been removed and listed underneath the paragraph. Insert the nine sentence-composing tools where they belong.

STRIPPED-DOWN PARAGRAPH

(1) All he could see was water. (2) It was June 23, 1943. (3) Army Air Forces bombardier and Olympic runner Louie Zamperini lay across a small raft. (4) Slumped alongside him was a sergeant. (5) On a separate raft lay another crewman. (6) Their bodies had **winnowed** [*shrunken*] down to skeletons. (7) Sharks glided in lazy **loops** [*circles*] around them.

—Laura Hillenbrand, *Unbroken*

SENTENCE-COMPOSING TOOLS

a. in every direction

b. somewhere on the endless expanse of the Pacific Ocean

c. drifting westward

d. one of his plane's gunners

e. tethered [*tied*] to the first

f. a gash zigzagging across his forehead

g. burned by the sun and stained yellow from the raft dye

h. dragging their backs along the rafts

i. waiting

After reassembling this paragraph, read it to notice the power that the sentence-composing tools add, with vivid details, elaboration, and style. Using sentence-composing tools in your own writing will also make it more powerful.

IMITATING NONFICTION SENTENCES

What are some things you learned to do by watching other people do them—like swinging a bat, making pancakes, buttoning your shirt or blouse, flying a kite, riding a bike? You learned probably by watching people and then imitating what they did.

Imitating is a great way to learn, including how to build sentences by imitating nonfiction authors who know—really, really know—how to build great sentences. Those authors you'll meet soon are your invisible teachers to help you build better sentences.

Sentence imitating uses an author's model sentence as a blueprint for a twin sentence. You build that twin sentence the same way the author's sentence is built, but you write about a different topic.

EXAMPLES OF SENTENCE IMITATIONS

Notice how each imitation sentence is built like the model sentence by the author. Their sentence parts are twins. After doing the activities in this section, you will be able to imitate sentences, too.

1. **Model:** When the ship was finished, it was as long as three football fields.

   —Will Osborne, *Titanic*

   Sample Imitation: After the bats had landed, they were as noisy as a chirping bird flock.

Twin Sentence Parts		
When the ship was finished,	it was as long	as three football fields.
After the bats had landed,	they were as noisy	as a chirping bird flock.

2. *Model:* I started making an iceball, a perfect one from perfectly white snow.

　　　　　　　　　　　—Annie Dillard, *An American Childhood*

Sample Imitation: He began examining the sick alligator, a still one with injured drooping tail.

Twin Sentence Parts		
I started making an iceball,	a perfect one	from perfectly white snow.
He began examining the sick alligator,	a still one	with injured drooping tail.

3. *Model:* The youngest and only boy of four children, Nelson Mandela and his father cared for the cattle and sheep.

　　　　　—Barry Denenberg, *Nelson Mandela: No Easy Walk to Freedom*

Sample Imitation: The distinguished and famous signer of the Declaration of Independence, Ben Franklin and his cosigners began this government and country.

Twin Sentence Parts		
The youngest and only boy of four children,	Nelson Mandela and his father	cared for the cattle and sheep.
The distinguished and famous signer of the Declaration of Independence,	Ben Franklin and his cosigners	began this government and country.

4. *Model:* In the back bedroom of a small house in Torrance, California, a twelve-year-old-boy sat up in bed, listening.

　　　　　　　　　　　—Laura Hillenbrand, *Unbroken*

Sample Imitation: In the tiny office of the accountant's space in the huge skyscraper, his broken computer turned on at night, flashing.

Twin Sentence Parts		
In the back bedroom of a small house in Torrance, California,	a twelve-year-old-boy sat up in bed,	listening.
In the tiny office of the accountant's space in the huge skyscraper,	his broken computer turned on at night,	flashing.

5. *Model:* With his free hand, he squirted the chicken's chest with alcohol, and plunged a syringe needle into its heart to draw blood.

— Rebecca Skloot, *The Immortal Life of Henrietta Lacks*

Sample Imitation: From the open hatch, Neil Armstrong stepped down the ladder with curiosity, and took an uncertain step onto the moon's surface to plant a flag.

Twin Sentence Parts				
With his free hand,	he squirted the chicken's chest with alcohol,	and plunged a syringe needle	into its heart	to draw blood.
From the open hatch,	Neil Armstrong stepped down the ladder with curiosity,	and took an uncertain step	onto the moon's surface	to plant a flag.

Imitating sentences is like filling in a picture in a coloring book. When you color a picture, you're given the shape for the picture, and then you add your own colors. When you imitate a sentence, you're given the shape for the sentence, and then you add your own words. In the following activities, you'll learn how.

ACTIVITY 1: IDENTIFYING TWIN SENTENCES

Choose from the sentence pairs underneath the model sentence the imitation of the model. Then copy the model and its twin to see how the two sentences are built alike.

EXAMPLE

> *Model Sentence:* When the work was done, the Titanic ship had cost more than $10 million, a **mind-boggling** [*huge*] amount in 1912.
>
> —Thomas Conklin, *The Titanic Sinks!*

SENTENCES

a. After the migration was complete, the Manx Shearwater birds had traveled more than 8,700 miles, a record distance for migration.

b. A widely used communication device, the telephone was invented by Alexander Graham Bell, a Scottish immigrant who received a United States patent.

IMITATION OF THE MODEL SENTENCE

a. After the migration was complete, the Manx Shearwater birds had traveled more than 8,700 miles, a record distance for migration.

Twin Sentence Parts			
When the work was done,	the *Titanic* ship	had cost more than $10 million,	a mind-boggling amount in 1912.
After the migration was complete,	the Manx Shearwater birds	had traveled more than 8,700 miles,	a record distance for migration.

Model One: Enchanted and enthralled, I stopped her constantly for details.
>—Richard Wright, *Black Boy*

1a. Friendly and obedient, the dolphin fascinated the marine biologist daily with its intelligence.

1b. Found worldwide, mostly in shallower oceans, dolphins eat mostly fish and squid.

Model Two: While she sat there, a fuzzy spider paced across the room.
>—Eleanor Coerr, *Sadako and the Thousand Paper Cranes*

2a. In the early afternoon, a groundhog began burrowing in the park across the street.

2b. After the Battle of Britain ended, British prime minister Sir Winston Churchill spoke about the Royal Air Force.

Model Three: Short, with a neatly trimmed beard and large, soft eyes, Nicholas hardly looked like the imposing ruler of Russia.
>—Candace Fleming, *The Family Romanov*

3a. Dignified, with a smooth white wig and confident, royal expression, George Washington ably served as the first president of America.

3b. Awarded a perfect score of 10 in the 1976 summer Olympics in Montreal, Canada, Nadia Comaneci was the first female gymnast to earn that score.

Model Four: My father, like most of the villagers, was a farmer and a hunter, depending on the season.
>—Quang Nhuong Huynh, *The Land I Lost*

4a. Mysterious primitive ancient statues, carved in stone, on a distant island in the Pacific Ocean have puzzled scientists.

4b. Sir Winston Churchill, like many of England's prime ministers, was a speech maker and a politician, never resting on his laurels.

Model Five: In the over two hundred fifty years since Ben Franklin invented the lightning rod, new uses for electric power have forever changed the way people use electricity.
—Rosalyn Schanzer, *How Ben Franklin Stole the Lightning*

5a. In an exploration throughout the universe after we survey the planets, incredible discoveries of vast importance will completely change the way humans perceive the world.

5b. In the unseasonably cold water off Cape Cod, a lifeguard saw what he thought might be a rock, but it turned out to be a freezing turtle that needed his help.

ACTIVITY 2: MATCHING TWIN SENTENCES

Match the twin sentence with its model sentence.

Model Sentences	Twin Sentences
1. Robert Oppenheimer dove deep into chemistry and physics in high school, and graduated from Harvard in 1925. —Steve Sheinkin, *Bomb*	**a.** The wolverine was eating lots of bones with internal organs and muscles still attached, a feast lasting many meals.
2. The idea that illness was caused by microscopic organisms, like bacteria and viruses, was not known in the 18th century. —Jim Murphy, *An American Plague*	**b.** A sea otter stored food always within its body and rolls in its skin, and ate from that supply for each meal.

3. Empress Alexandra was wearing a gold gown with thousands of diamonds and pearls sown into it, a costume costing ten million dollars today. —Candace Fleming, *The Family Romanov*	**c.** Cheering the victory of the NFL football team, the excited fan in a group of friends stood, his clothing marked with the team's purple color to indicate his loyalty.
4. Claudette Colvin's story is a story of a wise and brave woman, who, when she was a smart, angry teenager in Jim Crow Alabama, made contributions to human rights far too important to be forgotten. —Philip M. Hoose, *Claudette Colvin*	**d.** The belief that pimples come from excessive carbohydrates, like candy and soda, has been disproved by dermatologists.
5. Awaiting the arrival of the condemned Benedict Arnold, the **ghoulish** [*frightening*] figure of a hangman stood, his face **smeared** [*covered*] with black axle grease to hide his identify. —Steve Sheinkin, *The Notorious Benedict Arnold*	**e.** Dr. Seuss' history is a story of a creative and determined author, who, when he was a talented, unpublished author in New York City, wrote fantasies about human behavior too insightful to be overlooked.

ACTIVITY 3: IDENTIFYING IMITATIONS

Copy the model sentence and the sentence that imitates the model because it is built similarly.

> ***Model One:*** After Anne's death, her diary was turned into a book.
> —Ann Abramson, *Who Was Anne Frank?*

1a. During a solar eclipse, the sky is turned into total darkness.

1b. NASA after the moon landing was guaranteed funding from the government.

Model Two: After many dry days, a heavy rain fell on the desert.
—Brenda Z. Guiberson

2a. The landscape was changed forever after the eruption of Mount Vesuvius.

2b. After many failed attempts, a bright light came from a bulb.

Model Three: Across the wide Atlantic Ocean they came, European **emigrants** [*newcomers*], looking for a new beginning on American shores.
—Rosalyn Schanzer, *Witches*

3a. They were unequipped to make the journey, refugees who had no idea how difficult the long and dangerous trip would become.

3b. On the broad movie screen he stood, King Kong, towering over a young beauty on the skyscraper's ledge.

Model Four: Long ago, in a land known as Camelot, there lived many knights and ladies.
—Cindy Neuschwander, *Sir Cumference and the First Round Table*

4a. Before now, in a time without manufacturing, there grew many gardens and trees.

4b. There were lots of dinosaurs in prehistoric times, known mostly as predators.

Model Five: Maria was a town character, a fat middle-aged woman who lived with her old mother on the outskirts of town.
—Judith Ortiz Cofer, *Silent Dancing*

5a. Serena Williams became an important athlete, a young African-American woman who competed on the world's courts with unprecedented success in tennis.

5b. James Dean, a talented actor and handsome young man, died at age twenty-four in an automobile collision with another car driven by a man named, oddly, Turnupspeed.

ACTIVITY 4: UNSCRAMBLING AND IMITATING SENTENCES

Unscramble and write out the sentence parts to imitate the model sentence. Then write a sentence imitation built with the same sentence parts as the model. Write about something real—a person, a place, a thing, an idea, or an event you learned about on your own, in school, or on the Internet.

EXAMPLE

Model Sentence: The largest island in the San Francisco Bay, Angel Island has a long and varied history.
—Erika Lee and Judy Yung, *Angel Island*

SCRAMBLED SENTENCE PARTS

a. for the month of January

b. the birthstone

c. symbolizes a loyal and trustworthy friend

d. the garnet

Unscrambled Imitation: The birthstone for the month of January, the garnet symbolizes a loyal and trustworthy friend.

Sample Imitation: An electric car with a sleek design for luxury, the Tesla commands a steady and increasing popularity.

Model One: Contrary to popular impressions, **leprosy** [*a skin disease*] is not highly **contagious** [*catching*].
—Norman Cousins, *Anatomy of an Illness*

1a. are not always active

1b. geysers

1c. disappointing to Yellowstone's tourists

Model Two: When trucks began to replace horses and wagons, he scoffed at the idea, **labeling** [*naming*] the trucks a mere **fad** [*trend*] that would never last.
—Walter Dean Myers, *Bad Boy*

2a. worried about bad nutrition

2b. calling the trend a short experiment that would end soon

2c. dieticians

2d. after sugar started to sweeten snacks and cereals

Model Three: Alicia's father, a successful businessman, and her mother, a violet-eyed **cultured** [*educated*] lady, raised her to be **assertive** [*strong*] and **resourceful** [*independent*] and have a love of the outdoors and school.
—Allan Zullo, *Escape*

3a. a passionately intense journey

3b. Vincent van Goh's paintings

3c. showed him to be original and interesting

3d. and his life

3e. and have an eye for the natural and beautiful

3f. a famous collection

Model Four: Balloons have risen every year in the Thanksgiving Day Parade since 1928 except for two years during World War II when rubber and **helium** [*gas*] were needed in the war effort.
—Melissa Sweet, *Balloons over Broadway*

4a. were honored by the sudden darkness

4b. theater lights have stayed on every night in Broadway's theater district

4c. when national or international deceased celebrities

4d. except for solemn moments of mourning

4e. since electricity began

Model Five: In planning for a **siege** [*attack*], the castle's builder located the well inside the inner ward, reducing the danger that the castle's main water supply could be poisoned by enemies.
—David Macaulay, *Castle*

5a. that the shockingly colorful gown would be duplicated by others

5b. the woman's designer

5c. reducing the likelihood

5d. chose a fabric outside the lady's usual taste

5e. in planning for a dress

ACTIVITY 5: IMITATING NONFICTION SENTENCES

Compare how the model sentence and its imitation are built, and then write a nonfiction sentence built a similar way. Write about something real—a person, a place, a thing, an idea, or an event you learned about on your own, in school, or on the Internet.

---

1. *Model:* Hungry, cold, and miserable, Harriet finally fell asleep.
   —Dorothy Sterling, *Freedom Train: The Story of Harriet Tubman*

   Imitation: Handsome, talented, and unique, Elvis easily drew audiences.

2. *Model:* Before King George the Third was either king or the Third, he was just plain George, a bashful boy who blushed easily.
   —Jean Fritz, *Can't You Make Them Behave, King George?*

Imitation: Before Princess Diana of Wales was either princess or wife to Prince Charles, she was a kindergarten assistant, an unknown girl who dated occasionally.

3. *Model:* One of the highlights of Gabriela Mistral's life came in 1945, when she became the first Latin American to win the Nobel Prize for Literature, a very special award given to only one writer a year.

—Monica Brown, *My Name Is Gabriela*

Imitation: One of the benchmarks of Steve Jobs' accomplishments came in 2001, when the iPod became the first digital media player to use iTunes for music, an online media store developed by Apple.

4. *Model:* In early California, there was no foundry to make iron products, especially railroad tracks, no plant to make carriages, either horse-drawn or for a train, or one to make a locomotive or a gun or powder.

—Stephen E. Ambrose, *Nothing Like It in the World*

Imitation: In early twentieth century, there were no electric lights to light the streets, especially urban dark streets, no conveniences to help housewives, neither dishwashers nor vacuums, nor the possibility to heat a home or a business or office.

5. *Model:* A Chinese merchant with partnerships in a general merchandise store and a dried fruit business in and around Canton, Wong hoped to expand his business in the United States.

—Erika Lee and Judy Yung, *Angel Island*

Imitation: An Olympic oarsman with incredible stamina in rowing ability and a proven physical talent in and beyond gymnastics, Joe Rantz wanted to apply his talents to the rowing crew at the University of Washington.

YOUR TURN: IMITATING A MODEL PARAGRAPH

The two paragraphs that follow—a model and its imitation—are divided into sentence parts by slash marks.

After looking carefully at the model paragraph and the twin paragraph, write a triplet paragraph built the same way. Like the model and its twin, your paragraph should have the same number of sentences with the same kind of sentence parts. Build your sentences the way the sentences are built in the model paragraph and the twin paragraph.

Write about something real—a person, a place, a thing, an idea, or an event you learned about on your own, in school, or on the Internet. Use one of these topics or come up with your own.

- Boston Tea Party

- Gold Rush of 1849

- assassination of President Kennedy

- Apollo 11 landing on the moon

- explosion of the Challenger

- dust bowl of 1930

- Hurricane Katrina

MODEL PARAGRAPH

This describes the Great Chicago Fire of 1871, one of the worst nineteenth-century disasters in the United States, which killed 300 people, left 100,000 people homeless, and destroyed much of the business district.

(1) Sullivan **ambled** [*strolled*] down a stretch of land, / crossed the street, / and sat down on the wooden sidewalk. (2) Adjusting his wooden leg to make himself comfortable, / he leaned back against the fence / to enjoy the night. (3) The wind, / coming off the prairie, / had been strong all day. (4) While he pushed himself up to go home, / he

first saw the fire, / shooting out the side of O'Leary's barn. (5) Sullivan made his way directly to the barn / to save the animals inside. (6) The barn's loft held over three tons of hay, / delivered earlier that day. (7) Flames from the burning hay / pushed against the roof and beams, / struggling to break free. (8) A shower of burning **embers** [*pieces*] greeted Sullivan / as he entered the building. (9) The heat / was fiercely intense and blinding. (10) In his rush to **flee** [*escape*], / Sullivan slipped on the uneven floorboards / and fell with a thud. (11) As he struggled to get up, / Sullivan discovered / that his wooden leg / had gotten stuck between two boards / and come off.

—Jim Murphy, *The Great Fire* (adapted)

TWIN PARAGRAPH

This describes the sinking of the luxury ocean liner Titanic, *promoted as unsinkable by its builders, on its very first transoceanic voyage, resulting in the drowning of 1,500 people.*

(1) Frederick Fleet looked out from the crow's nest, / spotted the iceberg, / and hung on to the alert bell. (2) Calling officer James Moody / to issue his terrifying warning, / he looked out into the night / to estimate the danger. (3) The iceberg, / jutting out of the ocean, / had been moonlit all night. (4) When William Murdock learned of the iceberg, / he then made a decision, / putting suddenly the boat into sharp reverse. (5) The captain made an announcement quickly / to the passengers / to warn everyone onboard. (6) The luxurious ship / carried over 2,000 people on its first voyage, / terrified by the danger. (7) Buckling of huge metal plates / loosened metal bolts and walls, / starting to wash away. (8) A blast of freezing ocean / filled the ship / as compartments flooded it. (9) The flooding / was shockingly immediate / and deadly. (10) In his hesitation to decide, / Captain Edward Smith called for the ship's designer / and asked for his opinion. (11) As the

Titanic struggled to stay afloat, / the designer realized / that the damaged ocean liner / had become flooded with a deluge / and started down.

To help you build your sentences the way the sentences are built in the model paragraph and the twin paragraph, here are the sentences side by side from each paragraph.

Author's Paragraph	Twin Paragraph
1. Sullivan ambled down a stretch of land, / crossed the street, / and sat down on the wooden sidewalk.	**1.** Frederick Fleet looked out from the crow's nest, / spotted the iceberg, / and hung on to the alert bell.
2. Adjusting his wooden leg / to make himself comfortable, / he leaned back against the fence / to enjoy the night.	**2.** Calling officer James Moody / to issue his terrifying warning, / he looked out into the night / to estimate the danger.
3. The wind, / coming off the prairie, / had been strong all day.	**3.** The iceberg, / jutting out of the ocean, / had been moonlit all night.
4. While he pushed himself up to go home, / he first saw the fire, / shooting out the side of O'Leary's barn.	**4.** When William Murdock learned of the iceberg, / he then made a decision, / putting suddenly the boat into sharp reverse.
5. Sullivan made his way directly / to the barn / to save the animals inside.	**5.** The captain made an announcement quickly / to the passengers / to warn everyone onboard.
6. The barn's loft / held over three tons of hay, / delivered earlier that day.	**6.** The luxurious ship / carried over 2,000 people on its first voyage, / terrified by the danger.
7. Flames from the burning hay / pushed against the roof and beams, / struggling to break free.	**7.** Buckling of huge metal plates / loosened metal bolts and walls, / starting to wash away.
8. A shower of burning embers / greeted Sullivan / as he entered the building.	**8.** A blast of freezing ocean / filled the ship / as compartments flooded it.

9. The heat / was fiercely intense / and blinding.	**9.** The flooding / was shockingly immediate / and deadly.
10. In his rush to flee, / Sullivan slipped on the uneven floorboards / and fell with a thud.	**10.** In his hesitation to decide, / Captain Edward Smith called for the ship's designer / and asked for his opinion.
11. As he struggled to get up, / Sullivan discovered / that his wooden leg / had gotten stuck between two boards / and come off.	**11.** As the Titanic struggled to stay afloat, / the designer realized / that the damaged ocean liner / had become flooded with a deluge / and started down.

Children are great imitators,
so give them something great to imitate.

—Anonymous

NEAT INVENTIONS: INFORMATIONAL TEXT TIDBITS

Many inventions, when first presented as ideas, are considered ridiculous, impossible, the result of imaginative but unrealistic would-be inventors. For example, when the original horsepower for cars was, in fact, horses, when people heard about a proposed new kind of transportation that did not require horses, reaction was disbelief, even laughter at the ridiculousness of such an idea.

However, with time and gradual but eventual widespread acceptance, cars driven by humans replaced horse-driven carriages. The first cars were called horseless carriages. Many think future cars will be self-driven—no horses, no drivers, just sensor-controlled technology that propels and guides the car. Will they be called driverless cars? Is that idea ridiculous, impossible?

In this section, you'll learn informational tidbits about neat inventions that already exist, and some that are now only concepts like driverless cars. While learning informational tidbits about those inventions, you'll also learn more about how to build strong sentences the way authors build theirs.

CARS: FROM HORSE DRIVEN TO COMPUTER DRIVEN

First take a look backward. The first engines were dogs, oxen, camels, horses, and any other animals that could be trained to pull. Think Santa's reindeer. Animals transported people and cargo from place to place. Food was their fuel. Cleaning up after them was their owner's unpleasant responsibility.

Before wheels were invented, people built flat platforms or sleds that animals dragged along the ground. Around 3500 BC, with the invention of wheels, transportation became smoother, but still animal-driven, although animals required food, rest, and sometimes balked about moving. Think donkeys.

Over hundreds of years, creative minds attempted to put animal power into engine power. Henry Ford, who loved machines but hated horses, is credited with realizing that the future of transportation was a vehicle not dependent upon horses but upon engines.

With the arrival of cars, Ford's revolutionary idea changed the history of transportation.

The rise of a culture in which ownership of automobiles became typical was one of the most sweeping cultural and environmental revolutions in human history.

—Christopher W. Wells, *Car Country* (adapted)

ACTIVITY 1: IDENTIFYING TWIN SENTENCES

What sentence in the pair is the model's twin? It is about a different topic than the model but built like the model. Copy the model sentence and its twin, focusing on how the sentence parts are built alike.

Model One: The **transition** [*change*] to electric and driverless cars is the most important social development since the World Wide Web.
—Levi Tilleman, *The Great Race: The Global Quest for the Car of the Future* (adapted)

1a. Called the worst car of all history, the Yugo had a radio that sometimes fell out of the dashboard for no apparent reason.

1b. The connection between cars and road construction is a clear result of the Model T's success.

Model Two: In the fourteenth century, four-wheeled vehicles were not in common use in the world since two-wheeled carts were easier to build and easier to steer.
—Richard W. Bulliet, *The Wheel* (adapted)

2a. In the modern age, passenger cars increased in number in the United States because automobiles were affordable to buy and economical to maintain.

2b. Although Ford cars sold well since the introduction of the Model T, the Ford Edsel, introduced in 1958, considered ugly and overpriced, flopped.

Model Three: Cars are into the biggest automotive revolution since Henry Ford **debuted** [*started*] his assembly line in 1913.
—Katy Steinmetz, "Forget the Distant Future, Smarter Cars Are Already Here" (adapted) (*TIME*, March 7, 2016)

3a. Cities went through an unforeseen population shift because cars enabled population movement to suburbs.

3b. The VW Beetle holds the record for most cars of the same basic style ever produced, totaling over 30,000,000.

Model Four: From the very moment that Karl Benz's invention of the horseless carriage took the road in 1885, the automotive industry of the world began.
—St. John C. Nixon, *The Invention of the Automobile* (adapted)

4a. James Bond's typical car in the Bond movies was an Aston Martin DB5, sometimes equipped with an ejector seat, machine guns, smoke screen, and other gadgets.

4b. After the very first time that Henry Ford's creation of the assembly line produced a car in 1913, the industrial process of many manufacturers changed.

Model Five: While Google did not invent the self-driving car, it created the industry of self-driving cars by purchasing startups, hiring experts, and developing mapping and navigation technologies.
  —Jeff Goodell, "The Rise of Intelligent Machines" (adapted)
  (*Rolling Stone*, March 23, 2016)

5a. Because Henry Ford did not want an expensive car, he simplified the creation of the Model T Ford by eliminating frills, removing options, and choosing one color and body style.

5b. A movie featuring a fantasy car that floats on water and flies in the air, *Chitty Chitty Bang Bang* is an amusing children's film based upon a story by Ian Fleming, author of the James Bond stories.

ACTIVITY 2: ARRANGING SENTENCE PARTS EFFECTIVELY

Unscramble each sentence two times—one acceptable arrangement, and one unacceptable arrangement. Then jot down why the unacceptable arrangement doesn't work.

EXAMPLE

Scrambled Sentence Parts

a. as a young boy

b. such as watches and mechanical toys

c. Henry Ford

d. had always been fascinated by mechanical devices

Unscrambled Sentences

1. *Arrangement That Works:* As a young boy, Henry Ford had always been fascinated by mechanical devices, such as watches and mechanical toys.

2. *Arrangement That Doesn't Work:* Henry Ford such as watches and mechanical toys had always been fascinated by mechanical devices as a young boy.

Explanation

The first arrangement works; the one written by Michael Burgan in *Who Was Henry Ford?* The second arrangement doesn't work because the place where it mentions watches and mechanical toys confuses readers.

- -

1a. beginning the age of the automobile

1b. in 1885

1c. the first car to be sold to the public

1d. of Karl Benz in Manheim in Germany

1e. rolled out of the workshops
                    —Richard Sutton, *DK Eyewitness Books: Car*

2a. on highways and residential and other streets

2b. with regulations and market acceptance

2c. over half of the cars of the future

2d. supporting the presence of autonomous cars

2e. will be fully autonomous
> —Kati Rubinyi, *The Car in 2035*

3a. necessary for everyday living

3b. over the past many years

3c. from an unreliable machine

3d. to a low maintenance marvel of technology

3e. the automobile has grown
> —David Dickinson, *The Old Car Nut Book*

4a. the assembly line

4b. is rightly praised as the man

4c. Henry Ford

4d. and developed the key to mass production

4e. who created
> —Steven Parissien, *The Life of the Automobile*

5a. thanks to a semiautomatic transmission

5b. the Ford Model T car of 1908

5c. was thoughtfully engineered and for the time

5d. was free from many of the quirks of earlier cars

5e. was relatively easy to drive
> —Design Museum, *Fifty Cars That Changed the World*

- -

ACTIVITY 3: UNSCRAMBLING TO IMITATE A MODEL SENTENCE

Unscramble the sentence parts to imitate the model sentence.

On the Mark: Use a comma where it appears in the model.

Model Sentence: In fantasy, cars fly by magic, like the Weasley family car in the Harry Potter series, or by sprouting wings, like Chitty Chitty Bang Bang.

—Andrew Glas, *Flying Cars*

Scrambled Sentence Parts

a. like programmed drivers

b. like the imagined robo-cars

c. cars drive by themselves

d. in future

e. or by following computers

f. in the sci-fi comics

Unscrambled to Match the Model

In future, cars drive by themselves, like the imagined robo-cars in the sci-fi comics, or by following computers, like programmed drivers.

Model One: At the end of an F1 Grand Prix car race, the tires will be so hot that you could cook an egg on them.

—Clive Gifford, *Car Crazy* (adapted)

1a. the crowd will be so loud

1b. near the finish

1c. that you could miss

1d. of a NASCAR competition

1e. a shot from a cannon

Model Two: By the time the Model T, introduced in 1908, was withdrawn from production in 1927, this early mass-produced, low-priced car had sold an amazing 15 million cars.
—Michael R. Lemov, *Car Safety Wars* (adapted)

2a. driven by a knight

2b. at the time the gold limo

2c. was parked within the spotlights

2d. had become a famous celebrity symbol

2e. this luxuriously styled, extended-length vehicle

Model Three: Super cars are the stuff of dreams, boasting exotic names and **outlandish** [*strange*] styling, low shapes that hug the ground, **stupendous** [*impressive*] engines, and top speeds that rival those of light aircraft.
—Evo, *Supercars* (adapted)

3a. trying self-driving approaches and computerized controls

3b. future cars are the goal of manufacturers

3c. self-operating mechanics

3d. that compare with cars of the present

3e. and affordable prices

3f. small bodies that transport the passengers

Model Four: During the crash, not wearing my seatbelt, I flew into the steering wheel, hitting my jaw above my teeth, cutting the inside of my mouth, breaking the windshield as the top of my head slammed into it.
    —Diane Poole Heller and Laurence S. Heller, *Crash Course*

4a. not considering the expense

4b. increasing the safety when any part of the car crashed into anything

4c. reducing the number of fatalities

4d. protecting the passengers within the car

4e. using the research

4f. cars came with seat belts

Model Five: With self-driving cars, the computer is simply a better driver than a human, better at keeping its eyes on other drivers, better at maintaining a steady cruising speed and maximizing fuel efficiency, better at making quick adjustments.
    —Matt Vella, "People Shouldn't Be Allowed to Drive" (adapted)
        (*TIME*, March 7, 2016)

5a. a car is always a safer place

5b. safer at handling weather conditions

5c. in dangerous situations

5d. safer at protecting its passengers on the inside

5e. safer at avoiding an unexpected **impending** [*near*] collision and maintaining road traction

5f. than a truck

YOUR TURN: NONFICTION SENTENCES ABOUT CARS

Now that you have practiced imitating model sentences, write your own imitations. Here's how:

- Skim this section on cars to choose three model sentences to imitate.
- Copy each model sentence.
- Study how each model is built by focusing on its sentence parts.
- Then, after learning more online or offline about cars, write an imitation of each of your three model sentences.
- Make sure your imitations are built the way the models are built.
- Tell your readers in each imitation a new informational tidbit about cars.

ONE MORE INFORMATIONAL TIDBIT ABOUT CARS

Question: Why was the Model T Ford nicknamed "Tin Lizzie"?

Answer: In a championship race in 1922, a beat-up looking Model T its owner called "Old Liz" entered the race. Spectators thought it resembled a tin garbage can and nicknamed it "Tin Lizzie." To everyone's amazement, Tin Lizzie won the race.

In automobile terms, the child supplies the power
but the parents have to do the steering.

—Benjamin Spock

MUSIC: FROM PREHISTORIC TO ELECTRONIC

Music is organized sound for voice or instrument, delivered through infinitely varied styles: from the Beatles to Beethoven, jazz to hip-hop, opera to country—and countless others in the musical spectrum. Every person, past, present, and future, enjoys music. Every culture, past, present, and future, invents music.

The first invented instrument was probably a primitive drum, used to keep time and add rhythm to a caveman's sounds. From that first prehistoric caveman pounding on a hollowed-out log, the beat goes on, and on, and on, always with newly invented styles in the present added to favorite styles invented in the past.

> *Music is as old as the first human beings on the planet,*
> *and has been invented by every people on the globe.*
> *Wherever we find a people, however secluded or isolated,*
> *separated by sea or mountains from other people,*
> *there we find music and musical instruments.*
>
> —Joseph Mainzer, *Music and Education* (adapted)

ACTIVITY 1: IDENTIFYING TWIN SENTENCES

What sentence in the pair is the model's twin? It is about a different topic than the model but built like the model. Copy the model sentence and its twin, focusing on how the sentence parts are built alike.

Model One: Many musicians would rather compose, conduct, perform, and study music than analyze it scientifically.
—Donald Hodges and David Conrad Sebald,
Music in the Human Experience

1a. Before the twelfth century most music was monophonic, that is, without much harmony.

1b. All percussionists will surely strike, tap, bang, but accentuate melody not create it separately.

Model Two: Before music recording was invented and all music was live, music lovers might hear their favorite music just three or four times in their lives, but today we listen to almost anything we want at the press of a button.
—Howard Goodall, *The Story of Music*

2a. When Thomas Edison's sound recording was invented and all sound could be reproduced, music fans could play their favorite songs through a needle placed on a plastic disk, but now those records from the past are replaced with music recordings through digital sound.

2b. Musical purists debate whether analog sound is better than digital sound, but actually most recordings utilize both methods of sound reproduction, with a proper balance between the two to produce a clear, effective, and memorable sound that will please varied listeners.

Model Three: We study music history because it gives greater understanding of all music, past and present, including the realization that pop music intended for teenagers first emerged after World War II.
—J. Peter Burkholder and others, *A History of Western Music*

3a. In the 1950s, when rock and roll first began, it elicited from parents concern that its frenzied tempo had a harmful effect on young people, who moved on dance floors in what parents considered inappropriate ways.

3b. Fans like popular music because it provides wonderful entertainment for all people, young and old, illustrating the fact that music from one generation can also belong to later generations.

Model Four: The **lyre** [*small harp*] was invented by Hermes, a figure of Greek mythology, when he **surmised** [*imagined*] that the shell of a turtle, if used as a body of **reverberation** [*echo*], could produce the intended music.

—R. Murray Schafer, *The Soundscape* (adapted)

4a. Orchestra music is notated by a score, the written notes of music, wherein it dictates that the sound of the music, if played from the sheet music, will create the desired sound.

4b. Electronic music composers have found new ways to write music, differing from the traditional way of using a staff upon which differing note values inform musicians about such things as tempo, speed, and loudness.

Model Five: Thomas Edison, the inventor of recorded music in 1877, was so enthusiastic about that achievement because before then music was live and restricted to a few concert halls in the major cities and the homes of the very wealthy who could afford to hire musicians.

—Andre Millard, *America on Record* (adapted)

5a. Hundreds of years old, lullabies have appeared in almost every culture, soft songs designed to lull a baby to sleep through gentle lyrics and slow music composed specifically for that purpose, and the most famous lullaby, with lyrics actually a little frightening, is "Rock-a-Bye Baby."

5b. Portable recorders, an improvement on record players from earlier times, became so popular after their appearance because after then portable music devices were manufactured and sold to a large population in the United States and the world in virtually every country that could afford to buy them.

ACTIVITY 2: ARRANGING SENTENCE PARTS EFFECTIVELY

Unscramble each sentence two times—one acceptable arrangement, and one unacceptable arrangement. Then jot down why the unacceptable arrangement doesn't work.

EXAMPLE

Scrambled Sentence Parts

a. the invention of *do-re-mi*

b. that made it possible

c. in days instead of weeks

d. although it seems so simple today

e. to learn complex songs

f. was a revolutionary teaching tool

Unscrambled Sentences

1. *Arrangement That Works:* Although it seems so simple today, the invention of *do-re-mi* was a revolutionary teaching tool that made it possible to learn complex songs in days instead of weeks.

2. *Arrangement That Doesn't Work:* To learn complex songs in days instead of weeks, although it seems so simple today, the invention of *do-re-mi* was a revolutionary teaching tool that made it possible.

Explanation: The first arrangement works, the one written by Rick Beyer in *The Greatest Music Stories Never Told.* The second arrangement doesn't work, because it is unclear what was made possible through the invention of *do-re-mi.*

1a. occur in some species

1b. bird-song

1c. is predominantly a male activity

1d. between male and female

1e. although duets

> —Anthony Storr, *Music and the Mind*

2a. music storage power

2b. within the next few years

2c. in future,

2d. will be **virtually** [*almost*] unlimited

2e. with devices supplying a **terabyte** [*one million million bytes*] of storage

> —David Kusek and Gerd Leonhard,
> *The Future of Music* (adapted)

3a. of sound recording technology

3b. but with the invention of sound recording

3c. before the existence

3d. sounds were not **ephemeral** [*temporary*] but permanent

3e. sounds withered away

3f. existing only until the sound stopped

> —Jonathan Sterne, *The Audible Past* (adapted)

4a. either hummed or whistled

4b. on the first musical instrument invented

4c. a drum created by pounding one object

4d. prehistoric music was primarily vocal music

4e. with the hand or some object like a hollow log

4f. later **supplemented** [*added to*] by some sort of beat

　　　—Michael Miller, *The Complete Guide to Music History*

5a. since the story of sound recordings

5b. is **overwhelmingly** [*hugely*] dominated by the story of music recordings

5c. if you could gather all of the sound recordings that exist today

5d. recordings of music would be the **bulk** [*biggest part*] of that collection

5e. into one collection

　　　—David L. Morton, Jr., *Sound Recording* (adapted)

ACTIVITY 3: UNSCRAMBLING TO IMITATE A MODEL SENTENCE

Unscramble the sentence parts to imitate the model sentence.

On the Mark: Use a comma where it appears in the model.

EXAMPLE

Model Sentence: The invention of the piano around 1700 gave the musical world something for which it had long **clamored** [*wished*], a keyboard that offered **unhampered** [*unlimited*] musical expression.
　　　—Stuart Isacoff, *The History of the Piano*

Scrambled Sentence Parts

a. about which they could totally rejoice

b. brought young people a style

c. the arrival of rock and roll around 1950

d. a music that energized teen spirit

Unscrambled to Match the Model

The arrival of rock and roll around 1950 brought young people a style about which they could totally rejoice, a music that energized teen spirit.

Model One: I am a white American male who listened to nothing but classical music until the age of twenty.
> —Alex Ross, *Listen to This*

1a. in a cave in Germany

1b. is a reedless instrument

1c. that appeared about 35,000 years ago

1d. the flute

Model Two: After the introduction of iTunes in 2003, Apple's sales of iPods, introduced in 2001, **skyrocketed** [*increased rapidly*].
> —Steve Gordon, *The Future of the Music Business*

2a. widespread interest in this style

2b. after the invention of jazz in the late nineteenth century

2c. introduced in New Orleans

2d. multiplied

Model Three: This **propensity** [*tendency*] to music shows itself in infancy, is **manifest** [*evident*] and **central** [*important*] in every culture, and probably goes back to the beginning of our species.
—Oliver Sacks, *Musicophilia*

3a. can develop and strengthen at every age

3b. an interest in instruments begins with children

3c. in a talented player of an instrument

3d. and sometimes results

Model Four: Understanding the materials and building blocks of music opens many doors, doors that remain closed to those who cannot get beyond their **limited** [*small*] knowledge.
—Jack Perricone, *Melody in Songwriting*

4a. who have not yet discovered prehistoric written music

4b. problems that stay unsolved by archeologists

4c. presents many problems

4d. identifying the origin and ancient history of music

Model Five: In the history of recorded music, the **heart** [*essence*] of **contemporary** [*modern*] recording music has been the invention of multitracking, which records all of the instruments on separate tracks and mixes them later into the best sound.
—Jeff Strong, *Home Recording for Musicians*

5a. has been the harp of antiquity

5b. in the inventions of musical instruments

5c. and experienced great popularity

5d. which appeared all over the world in many cultures

5e. the oldest of string instruments

5f. during the Middle Ages (500–1500) and the Renaissance (1300–1600)

YOUR TURN: NONFICTION SENTENCES ABOUT MUSIC

Now that you have practiced imitating model sentences, write your own imitations. Here's how:

- Skim this section on music to choose three model sentences to imitate.

- Copy each model sentence.

- Study how each model is built by focusing on its sentence parts.

- Then, after learning more online or offline about music, write an imitation of each of your three model sentences.

- Make sure your imitations are built the way the models are built.

- Tell your readers in each imitation a new informational tidbit about music.

- -

ONE MORE INFORMATIONAL TIDBIT ABOUT MUSIC

Question: What famous song from *The Sound of Music* by Rogers and Hammerstein uses notes going up and down the *do-re-mi* scale?

Answer: Its title is "Do-Re-Mi."

- -

I would teach children music, physics, and philosophy, but most importantly music, for in the patterns of music and all the arts are the keys of learning.

—Plato

- -

PLUMBING: FROM OUTSIDE TO INSIDE

Since 4000 BC, water pipes have been a part of civilization used to transport water from outside to inside for drinking, cooking, and laundering. Ancient Egypt developed the first indoor plumbing for bathrooms for use inside pyramids. Over the centuries, gradual improvements were made to provide indoor plumbing to more and more people, but progress was slow. In 1950, in the United States, 75 percent of homes had indoor water, but 50 percent of rural homes did not, depending instead upon wells and outdoor toilets. Today, though, in the United States almost all homes have indoor plumbing.

We owe our way of life to Roman lead workers, to craftsmen who plumbed early European cities, and to the work of such men as Sir John Harington, inventor of the flushing toilet in 1597.

—W. Hodding Carter, *Flushed* (adapted)

ACTIVITY 1: IDENTIFYING TWIN SENTENCES

What sentence in the pair is the model's twin? It is about a different topic than the model but built like the model. Copy the model sentence and its twin, focusing on how the sentence parts are built alike.

Model One: Before the luxury of indoor plumbing, **outhouses** [*outdoor toilets*] were the rule, and they appeared in all kinds of designs.

—Dottie Booth, *Nature Calls*

1a. After the arrival of private bathrooms, tubs were a necessity, and they came in limited kinds of materials.

1b. The earliest water sanitation systems were devised by people living close to water in the form of a brook or a stream.

Model Two: The history of the bathroom in Europe and North America is a strange story of people who washed themselves often, sometimes, or not at all.
> —Patricia Lauber, *What You Never Knew About*
> *Tubs, Toilets, and Showers*

2a. The use of a stream in country and small settlements was a simple example of sanitation that worked always, occasionally, or not very well.

2b. Queen Isabella of Spain, the queen who launched Christopher Columbus on his trip to the New World, only bathed twice in her life.

Model Three: For many ancient Romans, bathing in huge indoor public bathtubs involved two or three hours of splashing, soaking, and steaming the body in water of various temperatures, then raking off sweat with a metal scraper.
> —Katherine Ashenburg, *The Dirt on Clean* (adapted)

3a. For most modern houses, washing in large downstairs washing machines accommodates four or five members of the family, cleaning and drying the bundles of clothes in several loads, then moving clean clothes to an upstairs bedroom.

3b. At some point in our history, our ancestors must have realized that water could be used not only for drinking and bathing but also for carrying away waste water from cooking, laundry, and toilets, requiring a drain system as a part of plumbing.

Model Four: When I was a little kid, there were no water heaters so Mother boiled the water for washing clothes outside in a huge black **kettle** [*pot*], heated underneath by fire from **kindling** [*sticks*].
> —Henry Skupin, *Growing Up on the Farm* (adapted)

4a. After anticipating a spa-like retreat in the hotel bathroom, I was disappointed to find nothing exceptional about the facilities, but just plain and ordinary bathroom fixtures.

4b. Although a water shortage was a huge problem, there was a faraway supply, so natives walked the distance for retrieving water miles away in the only available location, controlled strictly by monitors from the government.

Model Five: After the main water supply, controlled with faucets and valves, enters a modern house, a branch pipe is joined to a water heater, which brings hot water to fixtures and appliances throughout the house.

> —Editors of Cool Springs Press,
> *The Complete Guide to Plumbing* (adapted)

5a. The single most revolutionary product to transform many under-developed areas would be a toilet because it would eliminate bacteria that causes widespread infection and sanitize entire communities.

5b. When a dishwasher control, set with ease and precision, starts a washing cycle, a hot torrent is sprayed on the dirty contents, which cleans assorted plates and glasses within the machine.

ACTIVITY 2: ARRANGING SENTENCE PARTS EFFECTIVELY

Unscramble each sentence two times—one acceptable arrangement, and one unacceptable arrangement. Then jot down why the unacceptable arrangement doesn't work.

EXAMPLE

Scrambled Sentence Parts

a. and without water

b. without water

c. our planet has no chance to survive

d. people are incapable of life

Unscrambled Sentences

1. *Arrangement That Works:* Without water, our planet has no chance to survive, and without water people are incapable of life.

2. *Arrangement That Doesn't Work:* Our planet has no chance to survive, and people are incapable of life without water, without water.

Explanation

The first arrangement works, the one written by Mary Muryn in *Water Magic*. The second arrangement doesn't work because readers need to have the phrase "without water" placed earlier for the sentence to make sense.

1a. in our lives

1b. in our lives

1c. and also **unquestionably** [*certainly*]

1d. the most important substance

1e. water is the most familiar substance

— Charles Fishman, *The Big Thirst*

2a. per **capita** [*person*]

2b. people

2c. use about one hundred gallons a day

2d. worldwide

2e. who have indoor plumbing

— Art Ludwig, *Water Storage*

3a. drinking **contaminated** [*polluted*] water

3b. were the main sources

3c. throughout water's history

3d. and being exposed to **stagnant** [*dirty*] water

3e. and **abbreviated** [*shortened*] life spans

3f. of human illness

—Steven Solomon, *Water*

4a. about one out of every nine people in the world

4b. to safe drinking water

4c. live in a region

4d. while even more people

4e. does not have access

4f. where water demand is **outstripping** [*exceeding*] water supply

—Stuart A. Kallen, *Running Dry* (adapted)

5a. continue to operate silently day and night

5b. and flush down our toilets

5c. the miles of pipes that bring water into our homes from distant locations

5d. the treatment plants that insure the waste water we drain from our sinks

5e. doesn't **pollute** [*harm*] the local river

5f. and the **network** [*web*] of storm drains that keep the rain from flooding our homes

—David Sedlak, *Water 4.0* (adapted)

ACTIVITY 3: UNSCRAMBLING TO IMITATE A MODEL SENTENCE

Unscramble the sentence parts to imitate the model sentence.

On the Mark: Use a comma where it appears in the model.

EXAMPLE

Model Sentence: The terrible epidemic of the Bubonic Plague, called the Black Death, wiped out a large part of the population of Europe within a few years as a result of unsanitary living conditions.

——Morna E. Gregory and Sian James, *Toilets of the World*

Scrambled Sentence Parts

a. as a result of his water fascination

b. instead of a scientist in a second life

c. might have been a plumber

d. the career goal of famed Albert Einstein

e. considered a scientific genius

Unscrambled to Match the Model: The career goal of famed Albert Einstein, considered a scientific genius, might have been a plumber instead of a scientist in a second life as a result of his water fascination.

Model One: Water covers 71% of the Earth's surface and is vital for all known forms of life.

——C. D. Shelton, *Water*

1a. most of the country's houses

1b. at home

1c. for everyday conveniences

1d. and is essential

1e. plumbing inhabits

Model Two: Recently, Chinese archeologists unearthed a two-thousand-year-old toilet with running water, a stone seat, and comfortable armrests.
—Jane Powell, *Bungalow Bathrooms*

2a. provides a clean water supply

2b. tap water

2c. with constant reliability

2d. now

2e. a modern convenience

2f. and unappreciated luxury

Model Three: Plumbing and sanitation are the **offshoot** [*result*] of the science of irrigation, something that developed at least 25,000 years ago.
—David Hatcher Childress, *Technology of the Gods*

3a. all developed countries

3b. of the culture of choice

3c. things that characterize

3d. are the features

3e. water and cleanliness

Model Four: For more than three thousand years, understanding and management of drinking water from indoor plumbing have dictated the growth and health of human settlements.
—James Salzman, *Drinking Water*

4a. from inside plumbing

4b. bathing and showering with tap water

4c. through modern faucets

4d. for less than two centuries

4e. have governed the habits and cleanliness

4f. within today's homes

Model Five: The purpose of a sewerage system is the removal by water of all **sewage** [*waste*] from dwellings, and its disposal in a way that **renders** [*makes*] it not only **innocuous** [*harmless*] but, if possible, useful.

—William Paul Gerhard,
Hints on the Drainage and Sewerage of Dwellings

5a. is the clogging of drains

5b. and the cleaning of pipe in a way

5c. a time for a drain plumber

5d. but, if effective, clearer

5e. that makes it not only usable

5f. from tree roots inside underground pipe

YOUR TURN: NONFICTION SENTENCES ABOUT PLUMBING

Now that you have practiced imitating model sentences, write your own imitations. Here's how:

- Skim this section on plumbing to choose three model sentences to imitate.

- Copy each model sentence.

- Study how each model is built by focusing on its sentence parts.

- Then, after learning more online or offline about plumbing, write an imitation of each of your three model sentences.

- Make sure your imitations are built the way the models are built.

- Tell your readers in each imitation a new informational tidbit about plumbing.

ONE MORE INFORMATIONAL TIDBIT ABOUT PLUMBING

Question: Over a lifetime, how much time do people spend in a bathroom?

Answer: On average, people spend three years of their lives in a bathroom.

We spend a lot of time in the bathroom. When we need to use the toilet, we go to the bathroom. When we want to clean our body, we go to the bathroom. When we want to brush our teeth, shave, or put on make up, and get cuts or scrapes fixed, we go to the bathroom. For us, the bathroom is part of our everyday life. It is hard to imagine a time when many houses didn't have bathrooms.

—Penny Colman, *A History of the Bathroom*

COMPUTERS: FROM GIGANTIC TO MICROSCOPIC

When the era of modern computing began, computers required entire rooms with air-conditioning and weighed many tons. Since then, computers have become smaller and smaller, until people can easily carry a small computer in a pocket or purse in the form of a smartphone. That shrunken size has been the single most important development of personal computers. In an amazingly short time, yesteryear's mainframes morphed into today's minicomputers, with methods of computing and communication delivered though miniaturization.

Instead of hanging large on a household wall, now telephones are small and portable in pocket or purse. Instead of radios or stereos standing and immobile on tables at home, now small electronic devices take music anywhere. Instead of maps difficult and dangerous for drivers to use while driving, now GPS systems speak destination directions, turn by turn. Instead of invasive, painful surgery to diagnose or treat medical problems, now computers work with CT scans and MRIs to produce quick and painless results. Computer applications of every kind are everywhere—thousands of them.

The combination of computing and communications unleashed a flood of social change, in the midst of which we currently live.

—Paul E. Ceruzzi, *Computing: A Concise History*

ACTIVITY 1: IDENTIFYING TWIN SENTENCES

What sentence in the pair is the model's twin? It is about a different topic than the model but is built like the model. Copy the model sentence and its twin, focusing on how the sentence parts are built alike.

Model One: The computer and the Internet are among the most important inventions of our era.

> —Walter Isaacson, *The Innovators*

1a. In 1984, author William Gibson coined the phrase *cyberspace* to name the Internet.

1b. *Angry Birds* and *Angry Birds 2* are among the biggest app games of modern times.

Model Two: Boasting a brand name recognized by 55% of the world's population, the name Amazon.com became a part of the popular culture.

> —Robert Specter, *Amazon.com* (adapted)

2a. In all of human history, the computer revolution has been the fastest growing technology, with rapid changes in hardware and software.

2b. Weighing a large amount unbelievable to modern users, the original electronic computer was twenty-seven tons within 1,800 square feet.

Model Three: The sight of people hunched over their smartphones, constantly touching their screens, in parks, restaurants, schools, or almost anywhere, has become the iconic [main] image of modern life.

> —Timm Hogerzeill, *Smartphone Addiction* (adapted)

3a. The prospect of everyone attached to a personal computer, always scanning incoming information, in news, weather, social media, or anything important, has changed from science fiction to science fact.

3b. Steve Jobs, cofounder of Apple Computer, compared a computer to a bicycle of the mind because both a computer and a bicycle require a user or they are inoperative and useless objects without a purpose.

Model Four: The Internet was to the twenty-first century what the telephone was to the twentieth century, reaching into almost every aspect of global culture, from publishing to entertaining to socializing, with emailing or texting becoming an indispensable part of daily life.

    —Katie Hafner, *Where Wizards Stay Up Late* (adapted)

4a. The microprocessor has become to the computer world what electricity was to the preelectric world, governing every type of computerization, from GPS to word processing to social media, with smartphones and tablets influencing most communication in today's world.

4b. Cavemen used fingers and toes to keep track of quantities, but when they ran out of those digits, they invented tallying devices like scratches in dirt or paint marks on stones or markings on bones, or any object that could keep count higher than the number of fingers and toes.

Model Five: In his short story "Into the Comet," science fiction author Arthur C. Clarke wrote about stranded astronauts who used an abacus, an ancient portable computer, to plot their voyage home when their spaceship's computer wouldn't work because the Internet was down.

    —Dan Gookin, *Laptops* (adapted)

5a. Occupying 1,000 square feet and weighing thirty tons, the ENIAC computer, the first major computer, built in 1943 at the University of Pennsylvania, did more calculating in the ten years it existed than had all of humanity up until that time.

5b. With their fast-typing thumbs, smartphone texters send messages that rely on emojis, clever pictogram symbols, to convey their meaning when their written words aren't helpful because they don't capture emotion.

ACTIVITY 2: ARRANGING SENTENCE PARTS EFFECTIVELY

Unscramble each sentence two times—one acceptable arrangement, and one unacceptable arrangement. Then jot down why the unacceptable arrangement doesn't work.

EXAMPLE

Scrambled Sentence Parts

a. which deliver **relevant** [*appropriate*] results immediately

b. use Google searches

c. that the world gets information

d. every day billions of people

e. changing the way

Unscrambled Sentences

1. *Arrangement That Works:* Every day billions of people use Google searches, which deliver relevant results immediately, changing the way the world gets information.

2. *Arrangement That Doesn't Work:* Changing the way the world gets information, which deliver relevant results immediately, every day billions of people use Google searches.

Explanation

The first arrangement works, the one written by Steven Levy in his nonfiction account of Google titled *In the Plex*. The second doesn't work because readers need to have the phrase "every day billions of people use Google searches" placed earlier for the sentence to make more sense.

1a. that filled whole rooms

1b. or even whole buildings

1c. were **enormous** [*huge*] **contraptions** [*machines*]

1d. the computers of the 1950s

1e. and consumed the power of a **locomotive** [*train*]

—T. R. Reed, *The Chip*

2a. potentially [*eventually*] bigger, better, faster

2b. a human brain performs

2c. even outperforming it

2d. artificial intelligence in computers

2e. mimics [*imitates*] the way

—Kevin Warwick, *Artificial Intelligence* (adapted)

3a. contain computers

3b. many devices you would not think of as computerized

3c. which can be retrieved by a service technician at the time of service

3d. including modern vehicles with computers

3e. that collect information about a vehicles' diagnostics

—Lynn Hogan and Amy M. Rutledge, *Practical Computing* (adapted)

4a. with an operating system providing the **means** [*method*]

4b. a computer system consists of hardware (a machine)

4c. to operate the computer system

4d. software (programs and applications)

4e. and data (information)

—Abraham Silberschatz and others,
Operating System Concepts (adapted)

5a. Steve Jobs almost single-handedly introduced the world to the first computer that could sit on your desk and actually do something all by itself

5b. with a spiffy little music player called the iPod

5c. and funded and nurtured a company called Pixar

5d. revolutionized music and the ears of a generation

5e. that made the most amazing computer-animated movies like *Toy Story*, *Cars*, and *Finding Nemo*

—Karen Blumenthal, *Steve Jobs* (adapted)

ACTIVITY 3: UNSCRAMBLING TO IMITATE A MODEL SENTENCE

Unscramble the sentence parts to imitate the model sentence.

On the Mark: Use a comma where it appears in the model.

EXAMPLE

Model Sentence: A calculator is only a part of a computer, a machine that can store information and process it according to programmed instructions, which require a computer that can quickly perform great amounts of tedious arithmetic.
—Mark Frauenfelder, *The Computer*

Scrambled Sentence Parts

a. an inventor who did design them and make them with great precision

b. which needed 120 years that were actually spent

c. computer parts were invented in 1833 by Charles Babbage

d. researching them for modern computers

Unscrambled to Match the Model

Computer parts were invented in 1833 by Charles Babbage, an inventor who did design them and make them with great precision, which needed 120 years that were actually spent researching them for modern computers.

- -

Model One: The Apple Macintosh computer introduced the biggest leap in the history of computers, a computer controlled by a mouse.
　　　　　　　—Ken Segall, *Insanely Simple* (adapted)

1a. of technicians in the computer room

1b. the first actual computer bug

1c. a dead moth stuck in the computer

1d. caught the attention in 1947

Model Two: Like driving a car or riding a bike, the more you practice and use the equipment, the more comfortable you will be and the better able you will be to adjust to future models.
　　　　　　—Catherine Laberta, *Computers Are Your Future*

2a. the more amazed you will be

2b. in learning the computer story or studying its history

2c. and the more likely you will be to applaud the technological accomplishments

2d. the more you understand and see the progress

Model Three: The Amazon.com site is a **smorgasbord** [*wide variety*] of selection, featuring books, music, movies, tools, and more, even oddball items like an inflatable unicorn horn for cats.
　　　　　　—Brad Stone, *The Everything Store* (adapted)

3a. became the head of Google

3b. with their operating systems from Google

3c. overseeing Google Drive, Google Chrome, Gmail, Google Maps

3d. Sundar Pichai

3e. even Android phones

Model Four: Google succeeded in being the best Internet search engine in the world, quickly becoming the search engine of choice among savvy users because its results were so accurate.
—Eric G. Swedin, *Computers*

4a. quickly replacing the phone calls of previous generations

4b. the communication habits of many teens

4c. because its impact was so strong

4d. social media excelled in changing

4e. among steady users

Model Five: The **origin** [*start*] of the Internet is a project funded in 1969 by the Department of Defense, an experiment to link that department to military research contractors, including universities doing such research.
—John R. Levine and Margaret Levine Young,
The Internet (adapted)

5a. is a story starring Mark Zuckerberg

5b. by sharing profiles highlighting their strengths

5c. an attempt to create a dating site for the college students on campus

5d. the startup of Facebook

5e. in his college years at Harvard

YOUR TURN: NONFICTION SENTENCES ABOUT COMPUTERS

Now that you have practiced imitating model sentences, write your own imitations. Here's how:

- Skim this section on writing to choose three model sentences to imitate.

- Copy each model sentence.

- Study how each model is built by focusing on its sentence parts.

- Then, after learning more online or offline about computers, write an imitation of each of your three model sentences.

- Make sure your imitations are built the way the models are built.

- Tell your readers in each imitation a new informational tidbit about computers.

ONE MORE INFORMATIONAL TIDBIT ABOUT COMPUTERS

Question: Where did Microsoft and Apple begin?

Answer: Both started in a garage.

Invention is 1% inspiration and 99% perspiration.

—Thomas Alva Edison, holder of 1093 United States
patents for his inventions, including sound recording

FUN INVENTIONS: AN ASSORTMENT OF ENJOYMENT

So many enjoyable things result from inventions, like bubble gum, hopscotch, French fries and potato chips, computer games, animated and regular movies, Ping-Pong, musical instruments. The list is endless. What fun inventions do you enjoy? Jot down and share with classmates five inventions you enjoy.

Hearing yours, some of your classmates might say, "Really! That's no fun!" Obviously, people disagree on what is enjoyable. For example, some people love baseball, but others couldn't care less. Some people love computer games, but others think they're a waste of time.

Enjoyment, then, is the result of preferences. The Roman poet Lucretius said it best in this famous quotation: "One man's meat is another man's poison."

There's one thing, though, that all people enjoy. Everybody loves the sweetest invention: chocolate.

Far more than a dessert, chocolate is the basis of a worldwide business that yields annual profits of $83 billion. The average European eats 24 pounds of chocolate per year. In the United States, more than 11 pounds of chocolate are consumed annually by the average U. S. citizen.

—Kay Frydenborg, *Chocolate*

ACTIVITY 1: GUESSING THE MODEL

Imitate the three model sentences. Write an informational tidbit about any fun invention you enjoy. Then, with a partner, take turns reading your imitations to each other, and see if your partner can guess your model sentence.

> ***Model One:*** Chocolate has provided inventors and **entrepreneurs** [*business persons*] great wealth, archaeologists clues to the lifestyles of people of ancient times, and biologists insights into the evolution of animals and plants.
> —Kay Frydenborg, *Chocolate*

> ***Model Two:*** For many people, tasting just a small piece of chocolate can **trigger** [*cause*] many memories, maybe of their first Hershey's bar or that special cake baked for a birthday.
> —Maricel E. Presilla, *The New Taste of Chocolate, Revised*

> ***Model Three:*** All of Hershey, Pennsylvania, including the zoo, the **antique** [*old*] town, the amusement park, the streetlights, even the chocolate factory, is clean and neat and cheerful.
> —Michael D'Antonio, *Hershey*

ONE MORE INFORMATIONAL TIDBIT ABOUT CHOCOLATE

Question: What did the inventor of the chocolate chip cookie receive as payment for selling the recipe to Nestle Toll House?

Answer: A lifetime supply of chocolate.

> *Research tells us that fourteen out of*
> *every ten people like chocolate.*
>
> —Sandra Boynton, *Chocolate: The Consuming Passion*

YOUR TURN: MINI RESEARCH REPORT

Many toys were invented for purposes other than fun.

- Play-Doh was intended to remove wallpaper.
- Slinkies were for keeping objects from falling over during rough waves at sea.
- Seesaws were used in ancient Rome as instruments of death with victims on seesaws eaten by hungry lions.

Learn about the amazing origins of any one of the toys listed below, and write a report for a magazine titled *Toys: Strange Beginnings* to be published on paper or online (or both) for the enjoyment and education of readers. Choose one of these toys for your research report:

1. Lego

2. checkers

3. Barbie and Ken dolls

4. toy soldiers

5. Pet Rocks

6. Scrabble

7. Raggedy Ann

8. Wiffle ball

9. toy trains

10. windup toys

11. Mr. Potato Head

12. Monopoly

13. Silly Putty

14. Ping-Pong

15. Trivial Pursuit

16. Rubik's Cube

17. tops

18. remote-controlled toys

19. skateboards

20. hula hoops

DIRECTIONS

1. As you learn about the toy's origin, take notes to provide content when you draft your report.

2. Pretend you are writing your report for a magazine for readers of all ages who would like to know the story of your toy's origin. For most sentences, include sentence-composing tools like the ones you've learned.

3. Study this short report on the origin of Slinkies, written by a published author, to learn how he builds strong sentences and paragraphs. In your report, try to build similarly strong sentences and paragraphs.

Slinkies: Wire That Walks

In 1945, an engineer by the name of Richard James was hard at work in a Philadelphia shipyard. The U. S. Navy had hired him to invent a stabilizing device for ships. When a ship is plowing through the waves at sea, it pitches and plunges and rocks every which way. Richard's job was to come up with something that would counterbalance navigational instruments so they would be level at all times.

Richard believed that springs would do the trick. He tried all different types and sizes, but none of them worked.

One day Richard knocked a large spring off a shelf. Coil by coil, end over end, it descended onto a stack of books, then down to a desktop, down to a chair, and from there to the floor.

At home later, seeing the spring walk down stairs, Richard's wife realized her husband had invented a new toy. (150 words)

—Don Wulffson, *Toys!* (adapted)

----

4. Like the example about Slinkies, write several paragraphs and make your report between 150 and 200 words long. Title your report with the name of the invention as the main title, followed by a colon and then a catchy subtitle like "Slinkies: Wire That Walks."

5. Exchange your draft with peers for suggestions. Then use their suggestions to revise your research report to improve it.

6. Although you may use sources online and offline to get information, do not copy sentences from your sources. Instead, use mainly your own words and sentences to tell that information. If you use

some author's words, be sure to put quotation marks around them to indicate they are not your words.

7. Your teacher may ask you to list the sources that provided information. If so, be sure to follow your teacher's guidelines for reporting your sources.

If e-mail had been around before the telephone was invented, people would have said, "Hey, forget e-mail! With this new telephone invention I can actually talk to people!"

—Thomas Friedman

QUOTABLE QUOTES: ESSAY TIDBITS

An essay is a type of short nonfiction that gives an author's opinion about a topic. Most essays are long, but in this section you'll study bite-size essays called quotations. Often called *famous quotes* or *pearls of wisdom*, they express the author's opinion about a topic. Quotations can be funny, serious, or somewhere in between.

Just as you need physical food for physical strength, you need brain food for brain strength. In this section, you'll feed on brain food—quotable quotes—to nourish your mind.

> *Some essays are to be tasted, others swallowed,*
> *and some few chewed and digested.*
>
> —Francis Bacon

You'll decide which quotations should be just tasted, which swallowed, and which chewed and digested. Many in this section are really delicious.

ACTIVITY 1: CHUNKING BITE-SIZE ESSAYS

To taste these little essays, take a bite at a time by chunking them. The chunked quotations that follow are all about the same topic: *birthdays*.

A good chunk makes sense by itself; it tastes good. A bad chunk doesn't make sense by itself; it tastes bad.

Read each chunk to the slash mark (/) and you'll be able to see the difference between bad chunks (*left column*) and good chunks (*right column*). To read well, chunk well, and then take a bite to see how it tastes.

Bad Chunks	Good Chunks
1a. A smile is happiness you'll / find right under your / nose.	**1b.** A smile / is happiness you'll find / right under your nose. <div align="right">—Tom Wilson</div>
2a. Anything you're / good / at contributes to happiness.	**2b.** Anything / you're good at / contributes to happiness. <div align="right">—Bertrand Russell</div>
3a. Happiness is having a / scratch for every / itch.	**3b.** Happiness / is having a scratch / for every itch. <div align="right">—Ogden Nash</div>
4a. Some cause happiness wherever they / go, but others cause / happiness whenever they go.	**4b.** Some cause happiness wherever they go, / but others cause happiness / whenever they go. <div align="right">—Oscar Wilde</div>

ACTIVITY 2: FINDING GOOD CHUNKS

Read each pair of sentences a chunk at a time. For each pair, tell which has good chunks, and which has bad chunks. Important: Read out loud, and pause where each slash mark (/) occurs. If it doesn't make sense, the chunks are bad. If it makes sense, the chunks are good.

EXAMPLE

a. Three can keep a / secret if two of / them are dead.

b. Three can keep a secret / if two of them / are dead.
—Benjamin Franklin

GOOD CHUNKS: **b**

1a. Home is /where the / heart is.

1b. Home / is where / the heart is.

—Pliny the Elder

2a. Yesterday's home runs / don't win / today's games.

2b. Yesterday's home / runs don't win today's / games.

—Babe Ruth

3a. The best time / to make friends / is before you need them.

3b. The best time to make / friends is before you need / them.

—Ethel Barrymore

4a. Any kid will run any / errand for / you if you ask at bedtime.

4b. Any kid / will run any errand for you / if you ask at bedtime.

—Red Skelton

5a. It is only when they go wrong / that machines / remind you / how powerful they are.

5b. It is only when they go / wrong that machines remind you how / powerful they / are.

—Clive James

ACTIVITY 3: MAKING GOOD CHUNKS

The quotations that follow are hard to read because of bad chunks. Move the slash marks (/) to make good chunks. With your good chunks, you'll understand each quote much more quickly.

EXAMPLE

Bad Chunks:

A friend is a / gift you give / yourself.

Good Chunks:

A friend / is a gift / you give yourself.

—Robert Louis Stevenson

---

1. A rich man's / joke is always funny.

—Thomas Browne

2. It's kind of fun to / do the impossible.

—Walt Disney

3. Be / yourself because everyone / else is already taken.

—Anonymous

4. If at first you don't / succeed then skydiving isn't for / you.

—Steven Wright

5. If you're too / open-minded, your brains will fall / out.

—Lawrence Ferlinghetti

6. Letting your mind / play is the best / way to solve problems.

—Bill Watterson

7. To / avoid / criticism, do nothing, say nothing, be / nothing.

—Elbert Hubbard

8. Always and never are two / words you should always / remember never to / use.

—Wendell Johnson

9. Be who you / are and say what you / feel because those that mind don't / matter and those that matter don't mind.

—Dr. Seuss

10. The surest / sign that intelligent / life exists elsewhere in the / universe is that it has / never tried to contact us.

—Bill Watterson

ACTIVITY 4: MATCHING QUOTATIONS WITH MEANINGS

Match the quotation in the left column with its meanings in the right column.

Quotation: Part One (1–5)	Meaning: Part One
1. Ten soldiers wisely led will beat a hundred without a head. —Euripides	**a.** Love needs to be valued more than power for peace to occur.
2. If you think you can, or if you think you can't, you're probably right. —Henry Ford	**b.** If you try for something beyond your reach, you will gain from the experience.
3. When the power of love overcomes the love of power, the world will know peace. —Jimi Hendrix	**c.** Leadership is more important than the number of soldiers.
4. Shoot for the moon because even if you miss you'll land among the stars. —Norman Vincent Peale	**d.** Children benefit from responsibility.
5. If you want children to keep their feet on the ground, put some responsibility on their shoulders. —Abigail Van Buren	**e.** What you expect is what you get.

Quotation: Part Two (6–10)	Meaning: Part Two
6. Be a rainbow in someone else's cloud. —Maya Angelou	**f.** A good friend will tell you the truth.
7. The best mirror is an old friend. —George Herbert	**g.** Bring happiness to someone having a hard day.
8. Families are like fudge—mostly sweet with a few nuts. —Anonymous	**h.** Always try no matter what.
9. Try and fail, but never fail to try. —Jared Leto	**i.** Instead of following others, make a better way for them to follow.
10. Do not follow where the path may lead. Go, instead, where there is no path and leave a trail. —Ralph Waldo Emerson	**j.** Families have nice members but also some unusual members.

ACTIVITY 5: UNDERSTANDING QUOTATIONS

Choose the statement that means the same as the quotation.

EXAMPLE

Quotation: Try to learn something about everything and everything about something.
—Thomas Huxley

a. *weak*—Know important things but also other things.

b. *strong*—Learn a little about many things but a lot about one thing.

TOPIC: FRIENDSHIP

1. My best friend is the one who brings out the best in me.
   —Henry Ford

   a. My best friend is the one closest to me.

   b. My best friend is the one I'm best with.

2. Friendship is something that is cultivated.
   —Thalia

   a. Friendship happens naturally.

   b. Friendship needs care.

3. Friendship is a single soul dwelling in two bodies.
   —Aristotle

   a. Friendship is shared between two people.

   b. Friendship shares one soul between two people.

4. Friendship is like money, easier made than kept.
   —Samuel Butler

   a. Making money or friends is easier than keeping either.

   b. Unlike money, friendship can be made but not kept.

5. Suspicion is the cancer of friendship.
   a. Friendship cannot prevent suspicion.

   b. Suspicion is bad between friends.
   —Petrarch

TOPIC: SCHOOL

6. A child educated only at school is an uneducated child.
—George Santayana

   a. It takes more than a school to educate a child.

   b. Children receive education mainly at school.

7. We don't stop going to school when we graduate.
—Carol Burnett

   a. When schooling is complete, we keep learning.

   b. After we graduate, we are then educated.

8. The things that have been the most valuable to me I did not learn in school.

—Will Smith

   a. The most important lessons are ones we learn in school.

   b. The most important lessons are ones we learn outside school.

9. A good school teaches you resilience—that ability to bounce back.
—Kate Reardon

   a. It is important to learn how to succeed.

   b. A good education teaches you to keep trying.

10. Love is the best school, but the tuition is high and the homework can be painful.

—Diane Ackerman

a. Even though expensive and sometimes painful, love is the best school.

b. An expensive college has hard homework and costs a lot of money.

TOPIC: SMILES

11. A smile is a curve that sets everything straight.
—Phyllis Diller

a. Smiling makes things better.

b. Smiling avoids problems.

12. If you force yourself to smile, within a couple minutes, you feel happy.
—Dean Norris

a. When you behave like you are happy, you'll become happy.

b. Stop frowning, and then you will feel much better.

13. A smile is a good deed.
—Shari Arison

a. Smiles help others.

b. It is good to smile.

14. A smile is a facelift that's in everyone's price range.
—Tom Wilson

a. A smile is a way to feel happy.

b. Smiling makes you look better.

15. Most smiles are started by another smile.

—Frank A. Clark

   a. Smiles are catching.

   b. Smiles are pleasant.

TOPIC: LAUGHTER

16. Laughter is an instant vacation.

—Milton Berle

   a. Laughter helps people forget problems.

   b. Laughter is sunshine after the rain.

17. There is little success where there is little laughter.

—Andrew Carnegie

   a. Laughter makes friendship.

   b. Laughter encourages success.

18. Laughter is America's most important export.

—Walt Disney

   a. America gives the world comic entertainment.

   b. Laughter is important all over the world.

19. Laughter is the sun that drives winter from the face.

—Victor Hugo

   a. Laughter cheers and warms a person up.

   b. Laughter makes a cold person warmer.

20. Laughter is the closest distance between two people.

—Victor Borge

a. Laughter brings people closer.

b. Companionship requires laughter.

ACTIVITY 6: EXPLAINING FAMOUS QUOTATIONS

In your own words, write the meaning of each quotation.

EXAMPLE

Quotation: Absence makes the heart grow fonder.

—Thomas Haynes Bayly

Same Meaning: When someone you love is away, your love for the person increases.

1. Necessity is the mother of invention.

—Plato

2. A journey of a thousand miles must begin with a single step.

—Lao Tzu

3. It is always darkest before the dawn.

—Thomas Fuller

4. Ask not what your country can do for you. Ask what you can do for your country.

—John F. Kennedy

5. If at first you don't succeed, try, try, try again.

—William Edward Hickson

6. Be kind, for everyone you meet today is fighting a hard battle.

—Plato

7. People who live in glass houses should not throw stones.

—Proverb

8. I haven't failed. I've found 10,000 ways that don't work.

—Thomas Edison

9. Don't cry because it's over. Smile because it happened.

—Dr. Seuss

10. Believe you can and you're halfway there.

—Theodore Roosevelt

ACTIVITY 7: FINISHING FIGURATIVE QUOTATIONS

Each quotation that follows uses figurative language—the language of comparison. The beginning of the quotation is provided, followed by two endings for that quotation. Choose the better ending.

EXAMPLE

Failure is a detour, not

a. a speed zone

b. a dead-end street

—Zig Ziglar

Answer: The best finish for this figurative quotation is "a dead-end street" (choice b) because, although both answers compare failure to another kind of street, only choice b means that failure can be overcome to lead to success.

----

1. Big sisters are
   a. the crab grass in the lawn of life.
   b. the teachers of little siblings.

   —Charles M. Schulz

2. **Fatigue** [tiredness] is
   a. the best pillow.
   b. a good friend.

   —Benjamin Franklin

3. A waffle is like
   a. piece of toast with lots of dents.
   b. a pancake with a syrup trap.

   —Mitch Hedberg

4. A good laugh is
   a. sunshine in the house.
   b. fun for the laugher.

   —William Makepeace Thackeray

5. A friend is

    a. a person to hang out with.

    b. a gift you give yourself.

                       —Robert Louis Stevenson

6. Sometimes I feel as if life is a tuxedo, and I'm

    a. just a pair of brown shoes.
    b. merely a nerd in a tux.

                       —George Goebel

7. Books are as useful to a stupid person as

    a. a mirror is useful to a blind person.

    b. a hammer is useful to a carpenter.

                       —Chanakya

8. Victory has a thousand fathers, but defeat

    a. is a baby.

    b. is an orphan.

                       —John F. Kennedy

9. A book is

    a. a way to learn about topics.

    b. a gift you can open again and again.

                       —Garrison Keiller

10. When solving problems

    a. dig at the roots instead of just hacking at the leaves.

    b. put on your best thinking cap and get to work.

                      —Anthony J. D'Angelo

YOUR TURN: MEMOIR

A memoir is nonfiction that tells about the writer's memories. Choose one of the quotations about memories from the list that follows. Then write about a person, place, object, or event that shows the truth of the quotation.

1. To this day I have the fondest memories of my old toys.

                     —Michael Keaton

2. My earliest memory as a kid was I would always try to make my friends laugh in class.

                     —Justin Timberlake

3. There's things that happen in a person's life that are so scorched in the memory and burned into the heart that there's no forgetting them.

                     —John Boyne

4. The kitchen is the heart of every home. It creates memories of family. (adapted)

                     —Debi Mazar

5. I still love making hamburgers on the grill. Whenever I make them, memories come up.

                     —Bobby Flay

6. Happy memories become treasures in the heart to pull out on tough days.

—Charlotte Kasi

7. Memories of family vacations and trips and outings will never be forgotten by children.

—Ezra Taft Benson

8. Some memories are unforgettable, remaining ever vivid and heart-warming.

—Joseph B. Wirthlin

9. Most of us have fond memories of food from our childhood.

—Homaro Cantu

10. One of the best ways to make yourself happy is to recall happy times from the past.

—Gretchin Rubin

Directions:

1. Write about your quotation without actually including it in your paragraph. If you succeed, a reader should be able to guess what it is.

2. For most sentences, include sentence-composing tools like the ones you've learned. See the sample memoir that follows with **bolded** tools.

3. Exchange your draft with peers for suggestions. Also, see if they can guess the quotation about memories you chose to illustrate in your paragraph.

Sample Memoir

For her paragraph that follows about her memorable teacher, Jenny chose this quotation to illustrate: "Some memories are unforgettable, remaining ever vivid and heartwarming." Notice how much information, detail, and sentence skill the tools provide.

(1) I don't know what it is about the fourth grade, but almost everybody remembers something. (2) Maybe that year divides at the brink of approaching adolescence, **close enough to be hinted at in the air, like the smell of the ocean**. (3) **For me**, fourth grade was mostly about my teacher Miss Gettle. (4) **Quite tall, always wearing pink lipstick**, she appears in my memory. (5) **During recess on cold winter mornings**, she opened her long fur coat, and I stepped into the warmth. (6) Then she closed the coat around me. (7) **Despite those affectionate moments**, she once stood me in the corner for talking and laughing, **although we both knew I was too old for that**. (8) **For the sake of classroom management**, she had to pretend. (9) Her heart, **I knew**, wasn't in it. (10) **Anyway**, she herself once laughed uncontrollably at Craig Nelson, **who was crossing his eyes and wiggling his ears at the same time**. (11) Miss Gettle, **unable to regain composure**, had to leave the classroom and go to the hall. (12) Laughter, **like her warm fur coat**, was one of our bonds.

—Jenny Crocker

TOOLS BY POSITION

Important: Notice that each tool is a *sentence part*, not a complete sentence.

OPENERS (*tools at the beginning of a sentence*)

- For me
- Quite tall, always wearing pink lipstick

- During recess on cold winter mornings
- Despite those affectionate moments
- For the sake of classroom management
- Anyway

S-V SPLITS (*tools between a subject and verb*)

- I knew
- unable to regain her composure
- like her warm fur coat

CLOSERS (*tools at the end of a sentence*)

- close enough to be hinted at in the air, like the smell of the ocean
- although we both knew I was too old for that
- who was crossing his eyes and wiggling his ears at the same time

Clearly, using sentence-composing tools within sentences—openers, S-V splits, closers—strengthens writing. Those tools will strengthen your sentences, too.

What's important is that you have faith in people, that they're basically good and smart, and if you give them tools, they'll do wonderful things with them.

—Steve Jobs

POPULAR AUTHORS: BIOGRAPHICAL TIDBITS

A popular author is a writer who has written famous literature read by many readers. A biography is nonfiction about the life of a famous person. A tidbit is a small but interesting detail. In this section, then, you'll learn interesting details about the lives of five popular authors of famous literature.

Here's a preview: four of those authors use initials rather than first names, and the fifth author, instead of his first name, substitutes the word "doctor" even though he wasn't one. Without peeking, how many last names can you guess?

J. K. _____?

A. A. _____?

E. B. _____?

J. R. R. _____?

Doctor _____?

While learning biographical tidbits about their lives, you'll also learn more about how to build strong sentences the way they did.

You learned earlier that imitating how an author builds sentences is something you can do, too. Now, you'll learn how sentences in an author's paragraph are built, and then write twin paragraphs with your sentences built pretty much the same way.

You already know how to imitate sentences, so imitating paragraphs won't be difficult because a paragraph is just one sentence after another about the same topic. You will go slowly, and imitate one sentence at a time.

J. K. ROWLING: WILD ABOUT HARRY

J. K. (Joanne Karen) Rowling, the author of the Harry Potter novels, used just two initials instead of her first name to appeal to male readers, thinking initials suggest a male author. Fact is more males of all ages—from boys to men—read the Harry Potter novels than females.

Although the manuscript for the first Harry Potter novel was rejected by twelve publishers, after that novel and the rest to follow it were published, the books eventually sold 450 million copies, and the movie versions grossed nearly 8 billion dollars.

TWIN PARAGRAPHS

A twin paragraph is a paragraph built the same way as a model paragraph. In other words, a twin paragraph is an imitation of the way the sentences in a model paragraph are built.

Following are three activities where you build a twin paragraph for the model paragraph. Although the paragraphs are all built alike, the content is different. Each paragraph is about a different tidbit from J. K. Rowling's biography.

MODEL PARAGRAPH

(1) When she sat down with pen and paper and began to write about the adventures of Harry Potter, a smile crossed her face. (2) Her expressive eyes, framed by long wavy hair, grew even wider. (3) Her pen slashed across the paper like a lightning bolt. (4) In her mind, a door to

a delightful new world of imagination and wonder opened wide, and she was about to enter.

—Marc Shapiro, *J. K. Rowling: The Wizard Behind Harry Potter* (adapted)

ACTIVITY 1: MATCHING SENTENCE PARTS

Match the sentence parts from the scrambled imitation sentence to the same sentence parts from the model sentence. When you finish, write out the twin paragraph, focusing on how the equivalent sentence parts are built alike.

Model Sentence	Scrambled Imitation Sentence
Sentence One	
1. When she sat down	**a.** a darkness sparked her creativity
2. with pen and paper	**b.** with a child and no job
3. and began to write	**c.** and started to worry
4. about the adventures of Harry Potter,	**d.** when Rowling saw herself
5. a smile crossed her face.	**e.** about the responsibilities of single parenthood
Sentence Two	
6. Her expressive eyes,	**f.** inspired always more
7. framed by long wavy hair,	**g.** her creative mind
8. grew even wider.	**h.** fueled by those dark thoughts
Sentence Three	
9. Her pen	**i.** soaked into her mind
10. slashed across the paper	**j.** that darkness
11. like a lightning bolt.	**k.** like a needed rain

Sentence Four	
12. In her mind,	**l.** of horror and evil
13. a door to a delightful new world	**m.** in a flash
14. of imagination and wonder	**n.** and the dementors were about to appear
15. opened wide,	**o.** an entrance to a frightening dark presence
16. and she was about to enter.	**p.** became unlocked

ACTIVITY 2: UNSCRAMBLING TO IMITATE

Build an imitation of the model paragraph by unscrambling the sentence parts. When you finish, write out the twin paragraph, focusing on how the equivalent sentence parts are built alike.

On the Mark: Use a comma where it appears in the model.

> ***Model Sentence One:*** When she sat down with pen and paper and began to write about the adventures of Harry Potter, a smile crossed her face.

1a. on her commuter train

1b. Harry showed his face

1c. as Rowling became engrossed

1d. and began to think about them

1e. with characters and plot

Model Sentence Two: Her expressive eyes, framed by long wavy hair, grew even wider.

2a. enchanted by fascinating memorable characters

2b. raced even faster

2c. her rich imagination

Model Sentence Three: Her pen slashed across the paper like a lightning bolt.

3a. slowed along the tracks

3b. her train

3c. like a blown tire

Model Sentence Four: In her mind, a door to a delightful new world of imagination and wonder opened wide, and she was about to enter.

4a. a possibility for an uncharted exciting adventure

4b. became possible

4c. with the train's delay

4d. about wizards and magic

4e. and she was glad to arrive late

ACTIVITY 3: COMBINING TO IMITATE

Combine bolded sentence parts to build an imitation of the model paragraph. When you finish, write out the twin paragraph, again focusing on how the equivalent sentence parts are built alike.

On the Mark: Use a comma where it appears in the model.

Model Sentence One: After she sat down with pen and paper and began to write about the adventures of Harry Potter, a smile crossed her face.

1a. When the final novel came out amid publicity and enthusiasm, readers were ready.

1b. The novel was published **and promised to thrill**.

1c. The thrill was **with the end of the series**.

1d. Readers missed their hero.

Model Sentence Two: Her expressive eyes, framed by long wavy hair, grew even wider.

2a. Readers loved **Harry's fantastic adventures**.

2b. They were **punctuated with chilling scary events**.

2c. His adventures **became even more beloved**.

Model Sentence Three: Her pen slashed across the paper like a lightning bolt.

3a. The novel flew out of bookstores.

3b. It sold **like another record breaker**.

Model Sentence Four: In her mind, a door to a delightful new world of imagination and wonder opened wide, and she was about to enter.

4a. The final novel mattered **in readers' lives**.

4b. It marked **the end to the long-adored Harry Potter series**.

4c. The series was **of morality and magic**.

4d. It was now **closed down**.

4e. Readers read it **but they were sad to finish**.

YOUR TURN: NONFICTION PARAGRAPH IMITATION

Now that you have produced three imitations of the same model paragraph, write your own imitation of that model paragraph. After learning more online or offline about a nonfiction topic, tell information your readers might not know about any of these topics: *animals, culture, entertainment, health, history, inventions, media, pets, politics, religion, science, space, sports, technology, transportation,* or write a paragraph with a new biographical tidbit about J. K. Rowling.

MODEL PARAGRAPH

(1) When she sat down with pen and paper and began to write about the adventures of Harry Potter, a smile crossed her face. (2) Her expressive eyes, framed by long wavy hair, grew even wider. (3) Her pen slashed across the paper like a lightning bolt. (4) In her mind, a door to a delightful new world of imagination and wonder opened wide, and she was about to enter.

—Marc Shapiro, *J. K. Rowling: The Wizard
Behind Harry Potter* (adapted)

ONE MORE BIOGRAPHICAL TIDBIT

Question: What date do J. K. Rowling and Harry Potter share?

Answer: Both were born on July 31.

*Happiness can be found even in the darkest of times,
if one only remembers to turn on the light.*

—J. K. Rowling, *Harry Potter and the Prisoner of Azkaban*

A. A. MILNE: CHRISTOPHER ROBIN AND FRIENDS

A. A. (Alan Alexander) Milne took his inspiration for ideas for stories and poems from his own son Christopher Robin Milne, whose stuffed animal toys became the models for some of the most well-known fantasy animals in literature: Winnie-the-Pooh, a lovable, kindhearted bear who loves eating honey; Eeyore, stuffed with sawdust like all of the other animals, is rather gloomy but lovable, and keeps losing his tail; Tigger, resembling a tiger, is very bouncy, but always in a good mood; Piglet, tiny but brave, loves bright colors, especially balloons; Kanga, mother of Roo, is a kangaroo who tries often but unsuccessfully to teach Winnie to jump; Rabbit and Owl, the only two real animals, pride themselves in having brains, unlike all the stuffed animals.

TWIN PARAGRAPHS

A twin paragraph is a paragraph built the same way as a model paragraph. In other words, a twin paragraph is an imitation of the way the sentences in a model paragraph are built.

Following are three activities where you build a twin paragraph for the model paragraph. Although the paragraphs are all built alike, the content is different. Each paragraph is about a different tidbit from A. A. Milne's biography.

MODEL PARAGRAPH

(1) At the age of two, young Alan began to read, pleasing his father, while his older brothers struggled to do the same. (2) Alan could write before he was five years old and entered kindergarten. (3) Every morning, Ken and his governess, Beatrice Edwards, walked Alan to school, where he continued to develop his reading and writing skills

at a remarkable **pace** [*speed*], **foreshadowing** [*predicting*] his literary career.

—Paul Brody, *A Biography of A. A. Milne* (adapted)

ACTIVITY 1: MATCHING SENTENCE PARTS

Match the sentence parts from the scrambled imitation sentence to the same sentence parts from the model sentence. When you finish, write out the twin paragraph, focusing on how the equivalent sentence parts are built alike.

Model Sentence	Scrambled Imitation Sentence
Sentence One	
1. At the age of two,	**a.** talented Milne started to write
2. young Alan began to read,	**b.** entertaining his child
3. pleasing his father,	**c.** from his fascination with children
4. while his older brothers	**d.** started to influence his writing
5. struggled to do the same.	**e.** as his young son
Sentence Two	
6. Alan could write	**f.** and invented games
7. before he was five years old	**g.** as he was always a clever boy
8. and entered kindergarten.	**h.** Christopher Robin would play
Sentence Three	
9. Every morning,	**i.** reflecting his son's toys
10. Ken and his governess, Beatrice Edwards,	**j.** inspired Milne to creativity
11. walked Alan to school,	**k.** Christopher and his stuffed bear, Winnie the Pooh
12. where he continued to develop his reading and writing skills at a remarkable pace,	**l.** every day
13. **foreshadowing** [*previewing*] his literary career.	**m.** while Milne began to write his stories and poems about toy animals

ACTIVITY 2: UNSCRAMBLING TO IMITATE

Build an imitation of the model paragraph by unscrambling the sentence parts. When you finish, write out the twin paragraph, focusing on how the equivalent sentence parts are built alike.

On the Mark: Use a comma where it appears in the model.

> ***Model Sentence One:*** At the age of two, young Alan began to read, pleasing his father, while his older brothers struggled to do the same.

1a. surprising its author

1b. failed to do as well

1c. when Milne's serious plays and novels

1d. in the world of children's literature

1e. *Winnie the Pooh* began to sell

> ***Model Sentence Two:*** Alan could write before he was five years old and entered kindergarten.

2a. after *Winnie the Pooh* was published

2b. and achieved success

2c. sales did skyrocket

> ***Model Sentence Three:*** Every morning, Ken and his governess, Beatrice Edwards, walked Alan to school, where he continued to develop his reading and writing skills at a remarkable pace, foreshadowing his literary career.

3a. earned money for Milne

3b. while *Pooh* continues to enchant readers and movie audiences through their worldwide reputation

3c. every year

3d. *Winnie the Pooh* and its sequel, *House at Pooh Corner*

3e. equaling Mickey Mouse's fame

ACTIVITY 3: COMBINING TO IMITATE

Combine bolded sentence parts to build an imitation of the model paragraph. When you finish, write out the twin paragraph, again focusing on how the equivalent sentence parts are built alike.

On the Mark: Use a comma where it appears in the model.

Model Sentence One: At the age of two, young Alan began to read, pleasing his father, while his older brothers struggled to do the same.

1a. In the first world war, A. A. Milne did something.

1b. He **returned to England**.

1c. His return was **ending his service**.

1d. Until the military intelligence his service was ended.

1e. They **hired him**.

1f. To write propaganda was the reason he was hired.

Model Sentence Two: Alan could write before he was five years old and entered kindergarten.

2a. Alan had done something before he was a soldier.

2b. He **had written**.

2c. He did it **before he was a soldier** and wounded overseas.

2d. He wrote before he was a soldier **and wounded overseas**.

Model Sentence Three: Every morning, Ken and his governess, Beatrice Edwards, walked Alan to school, where he continued to develop his reading and writing skills at a remarkable pace, foreshadowing his literary career.

3a. Later on, something changed.

3b. Milne and fellow pacifists did something.

3c. They became **antiwar activists**.

3d. They **denounced war in general**.

3e. They denounced it **because it aimed to end lives**.

3f. It aimed to end lives **and hopeful futures**.

3g. In a bloody carnage is how those endings would happen.

3h. The carnage would wind up **claiming so many young soldiers**.

YOUR TURN: NONFICTION PARAGRAPH IMITATION

Now that you have produced three imitations of the same model paragraph, write your own imitation of that model paragraph. After learning more online or offline about a nonfiction topic, tell information your readers might not know about any of these topics: *animals, culture, entertainment, health, history, inventions, media, pets, politics, religion, science, space, sports, technology, transportation,* or write a paragraph with a new biographical tidbit about A. A. Milne.

MODEL PARAGRAPH

(1) At the age of two, young Alan began to read, pleasing his father, while his older brothers struggled to do the same. (2) Alan could write before he was five years old and entered kindergarten. (3) Every morning, Ken and his governess, Beatrice Edwards, walked Alan to

school, where he continued to develop his reading and writing skills at a remarkable **pace** [*speed*], **foreshadowing** [*predicting*] his literary career.

—Paul Brody, *A Biography of A. A. Milne* (adapted)

ONE MORE BIOGRAPHICAL TIDBIT

Question: How much money does the Walt Disney Company make each year on their Winnie the Pooh merchandise?

Answer: In addition to money from Disney's Winnie the Pooh movies, each year Disney's Winnie the Pooh merchandise brings in billions of dollars, second in dollars only to Disney's Mickey Mouse merchandise.

You are braver than you believe, stronger than you seem, and smarter than you think.

—A. A. Milne, *The House at Pooh Corner*

E. B. WHITE: A BELOVED PIG AND SPIDER

E. B. (Elwyn Brooks) White wrote *Charlotte's Web*, a story of love between Wilbur the pig and Charlotte the spider. That novel is one of the most beloved stories of all time. Its author lived on a farm with many kinds of animals—including pigs and spiders—where he studied how they lived with great intensity and affection. He spent a year studying the lives of spiders on that farm in preparation for writing *Charlotte's Web*. It is available worldwide in over thirty-five languages, selling many millions of copies. According to polls of librarians, teachers, and publishers, *Charlotte's Web* ranks as the best children's book ever published in the United States. E. B. White's other children's novels—*Stuart Little* and *The Trumpet of the Swan*—also rank in the top 100 best-selling children's books.

Every day somewhere in the world, countless children and adults are opening the book and turning to the first page and reading in English or Norwegian or Chinese or Braille the opening of the book: "'Where's Papa going with that ax?' said Fern to her mother as they were setting the table for breakfast."

—Michael Sims, *The Story of Charlotte's Web: E. B. White's Eccentric Life in Nature and the Birth of an American Classic*

TWIN PARAGRAPHS

A twin paragraph is a paragraph built the same way as a model paragraph. In other words, a twin paragraph is an imitation of the way the sentences in a model paragraph are built.

Following are three activities where you build a twin paragraph for the model paragraph. Although the paragraphs are all built alike, the content is different. Each paragraph is about a different tidbit from E. B. White's biography.

MODEL PARAGRAPH

(1) While he was sick in bed, a fearless young house mouse visited the child Elwyn in his bedroom and was interested enough in this large but quiet neighbor to gradually become a tamed pet. (2) Elwyn supplied the mouse with a little house and watched closely as the mouse explored with its tiny paws and turned its dark eyes to look up at the boy. (3) He even taught it several tricks.

—Michael Sims, *The Story of Charlotte's Web* (adapted)

ACTIVITY 1: MATCHING SENTENCE PARTS

Match the sentence parts from the scrambled imitation sentence to the same sentence parts from the model sentence. When you finish, write out the twin paragraph, focusing on how the equivalent sentence parts are built alike.

Model Sentence	Scrambled Imitation Sentence
Sentence One	
1. While he was sick in bed,	a. to eventually become White's literary setting
2. a fearless young house mouse	b. attracted the young Elwyn through his curiosity and was magnetic enough
3. visited the child Elwyn in his bedroom and was interested enough	c. a nearby appealing large barn
4. in this large but quiet neighbor	d. when he was still in childhood
5. to gradually become a tamed pet	e. in this special and appealing place

Sentence Two	
6. Elwyn supplied the mouse	**f.** and remembered clearly
7. with a little house	**g.** White recalled the barn
8. and watched closely	**h.** with a literary interest
9. as the mouse explored with its tiny paws	**i.** when the barn filled with many fascinating animals
10. and turned its dark eyes to look up at the boy.	**j.** and inspired White's vivid imagination to play around in a story
Sentence Three	
11. He even	**k.** great luck
12. taught it	**l.** considered the barn
13. several tricks.	**m.** E. B. White always

ACTIVITY 2: UNSCRAMBLING TO IMITATE

Build an imitation of the model paragraph by unscrambling the sentence parts. When you finish, write out the twin paragraph, focusing on how the equivalent sentence parts are built alike.

On the Mark: Use a comma where it appears in the model.

> ***Model Sentence One:*** While he was sick in bed, a fearless young house mouse visited the child Elwyn in his bedroom and was interested enough in this large but quiet neighbor to gradually become a tamed pet.
>
> **1a.** a soft, furry big-eyed bunny greeted the child in its hutch
>
> **1b.** and was tame enough
>
> **1c.** to always welcome the little boy
>
> **1d.** while Elwyn was growing up on a farm
>
> **1e.** in this safe and protected environment

Model Sentence Two: Elwyn supplied the mouse with a little house and watched closely as the mouse explored with its tiny paws and turned its dark eyes to look up at the boy.

2a. and learned quickly

2b. Elwyn tended various animals with a gentle hand

2c. as he observed with an intense interest

2d. to store away for new stories

2e. and studied the animals' behaviors

Model Sentence Three: He even taught it several tricks.

3a. special treats

3b. he

3c. often brought them

ACTIVITY 3: COMBINING TO IMITATE

Combine bolded sentence parts to build an imitation of the model paragraph. When you finish, write out the twin paragraph, again focusing on how the equivalent sentence parts are built alike.

On the Mark: Use a comma where it appears in the model.

Model Sentence One: While he was sick in bed, a fearless young house mouse visited the child Elwyn in his bedroom and was interested enough in this large but quiet neighbor to gradually become a tamed pet.

1a. While Elwyn was still a toddler, he got something.

1b. It was **a fascinating new chicken incubator.**

1c. The incubator **entertained the child in his backyard on his farm.**

1d. It was entertaining **and was effective enough**.

1e. In this quiet but friendly environment it was entertaining and effective.

1f. It was effective enough **to eventually hatch forty-seven eggs**.

Model Sentence Two: Elwyn supplied the mouse with a little house and watched closely as the mouse explored with its tiny paws and turned its dark eyes to look up at the boy.

2a. A farmhand placed the remaining three somewhere.

2b. On a manure pile is where he placed them.

2c. He placed them **and explained carefully** something.

2d. As the boy worried about their hatching the farmhand gave him an explanation.

2e. He explained **and repeated his advice**.

2f. To wait patiently was his direction.

2g. For their hatching was what the child should wait for.

Model Sentence Three: He even taught it several tricks.

3a. The child closely watched.

3b. The eggs did something.

3c. They had a **surprise hatching**.

YOUR TURN: NONFICTION PARAGRAPH IMITATION

Now that you have produced three imitations of the same model paragraph, write your own imitation of that model paragraph. After learning more online or offline about a nonfiction topic, tell information your readers might not know about any of these topics: *animals, culture, entertainment, health, history, inventions, media, pets, politics, religion, science, space, sports, technology, transportation,* or write a paragraph with a new biographical tidbit about E. B. White.

MODEL PARAGRAPH

(1) While he was sick in bed, a fearless young house mouse visited the child Elwyn in his bedroom and was interested enough in this large but quiet neighbor to gradually become a tamed pet. (2) Elwyn supplied the mouse with a little house and watched closely as the mouse explored with its tiny paws and turned its dark eyes to look up at the boy. (3) He even taught it several tricks.

—Michael Sims, *The Story of Charlotte's Web* (adapted)

ONE MORE BIOGRAPHICAL TIDBIT

Question: Although E. B. White's real first name was Elwyn, which he disliked, what was his nickname in college?

Answer: Students at Cornell University whose last name was the same as the last name of Cornell's founder Andrew Dickson White were nicknamed "Andy," a name E. B. White kept for the rest of his life.

You have been my friend.
That in itself is a tremendous thing.

—E. B. White, *Charlotte's Web*

J. R. R. TOLKIEN: LORD OF THE FANTASIES

J. R. R. (John Ronald Ruel) Tolkien, the father of fantasy literature through his novels *The Hobbit* and the Lord of the Rings trilogy, was a precocious child who could read and write fluently at age four. A highly productive writer, the adult Tolkien wrote his 200,000-word novel *The Lord of the Rings*. His publisher, noting the high cost of paper in England after World War I, broke it into three separate novels to reduce production costs. Those three novels were published separately over several years: *The Fellowship of the Ring*, *The Two Towers*, and *The Return of the King*.

Tolkien's books have sold over a combined total of 250 million copies, have been made into award-winning films, and continue to enchant new generations of readers fascinated by their adventurous fantasies. Tolkien ranks in the top five best-selling authors from those no longer alive.

TWIN PARAGRAPHS

A twin paragraph is a paragraph built the same way as a model paragraph. In other words, a twin paragraph is an imitation of the way the sentences in a model paragraph are built.

Following are three activities where you build a twin paragraph for the model paragraph. Although the paragraphs are all built alike, the content is different. Each paragraph is about a different tidbit from J. R. R. Tolkien's biography.

MODEL PARAGRAPH

(1) When Ronald was beginning to walk, he stumbled on a **tarantula** [*large hairy spider*]. (2) It bit him, and he ran in terror until the nurse snatched him up and sucked out the poison. (3) When he

grew up, he could remember running in fear through long, dead grass. (4) In his stories, Tolkien wrote more than once of monstrous spiders with **venomous** [*poisonous*] bites.

—Humphrey Carpenter, *J. R. R. Tolkien: A Biography* (adapted)

ACTIVITY 1: MATCHING SENTENCE PARTS

Match the sentence parts from the scrambled imitation sentence to the same sentence parts from the model sentence. When you finish, write out the twin paragraph, focusing on how the equivalent sentence parts are built alike.

Model Sentence	Scrambled Imitation Sentence
Sentence One	
1. When Ronald	**a.** he joined
2. was beginning to walk,	**b.** with a group
3. he stumbled	**c.** as Tolkien
4. on a tarantula.	**d.** was continuing to write
Sentence Two	
5. It bit him,	**e.** and brought out his best
6. and he ran in terror	**f.** the members encouraged him
7. until the nurse snatched him up	**g.** and Tolkien bonded with them
8. and sucked out the poison.	**h.** as the group praised him highly
Sentence Three	
9. When he grew up,	**i.** with intense, careful attention
10. he could remember	**j.** listening to the group
11. running in fear	**k.** when he sat down
12. through long, dead grass.	**l.** he would enjoy
Sentence Four	
13. In his stories,	**m.** of comparable talent
14. Tolkien wrote more than once	**n.** among the members
15. of monstrous spiders	**o.** with similar taste
16. with venomous bites.	**p.** Tolkien found more than one

ACTIVITY 2: UNSCRAMBLING TO IMITATE

Build an imitation of the model paragraph by unscrambling the sentence parts. When you finish, write out the twin paragraph, focusing on how the equivalent sentence parts are built alike.

On the Mark: Use a comma where it appears in the model.

> ***Model Sentence One:*** When Ronald was beginning to walk, he stumbled on a tarantula.

1a. with yearly letters

1b. he entertained

1c. when Tolkien was learning to parent

> ***Model Sentence Two:*** It bit him, and he ran in terror until the nurse snatched him up and sucked out the poison.

2a. because his children enjoyed

2b. and loved letters near each Christmas

2c. they portrayed Father Christmas

2d. Father Christmas' adventures

2e. and Tolkien wrote with pride

> ***Model Sentence Three:*** When he grew up, he could remember running in fear through long, dead grass.

3a. he would illustrate

3b. against scary, ugly goblins

3c. when Tolkien wrote each

3d. fighting for Father Christmas

Model Sentence Four: In his stories, Tolkien wrote more than once of monstrous spiders with venomous bites.

4a. with the North Polar Bear

4b. in yearly letters

4c. among Father Christmas' helpers

4d. Tolkien entertained his four children

ACTIVITY 3: COMBINING TO IMITATE

Combine bolded sentence parts to build an imitation of the model sentence. When you finish, write out the twin paragraph, focusing on how the equivalent sentence parts are built alike.

On the Mark: Use a comma where it appears in the model.

Model Sentence One: When Ronald was beginning to walk, he stumbled on a tarantula.

1a. When World War II was starting to emerge, Tolkien had a job.

1b. It was an occupation at which **Tolkien worked**.

1c. He worked **as a spy**.

Model Sentence Two: It bit him, and he ran in terror until the nurse snatched him up and sucked out the poison.

2a. As a matter of fact, **the job suited him**.

2b. It was an appropriate job, **and he trained as a code-breaker**.

2c. That was **before the government** did something to Tolkien.

2d. What it did was **let him go**.

2e. It did that **and released him from the Foreign Service**.

Model Sentence Three: When he grew up, he could remember running in fear through long, dead grass.

3a. Something happened **when he started again**.

3b. He would continue was what Tolkien decided.

3c. The continuing was **writing with stories**.

3d. Toward eventual, successful publication was his aim.

Model Sentence Four: In his stories, Tolkien wrote more than once of monstrous spiders with venomous bites.

4a. On his trilogy he worked.

4b. His accomplishment was that **Tolkien wrote throughout those stories**.

4c. In various forms throughout them he wrote.

4d. Those forms were **of high fantasy**.

YOUR TURN: NONFICTION PARAGRAPH IMITATION

Now that you have produced three imitations of the same model paragraph, write your own imitation of that model paragraph. After learning more online or offline about a nonfiction topic, tell information your readers might not know about any of these topics: *animals, culture, entertainment, health, history, inventions, media, pets, politics, religion, science, space, sports, technology, transportation,* or write a paragraph with a new biographical tidbit about J. R. R. Tolkien.

MODEL PARAGRAPH

(1) When Ronald was beginning to walk, he stumbled on a tarantula. (2) It bit him, and he ran in terror until the nurse snatched him up and sucked out the poison. (3) When he grew up, he could

remember running in fear through long, dead grass. (4) In his stories, Tolkien wrote more than once of monstrous spiders with venomous bites.

—Humphrey Carpenter, *J. R. R. Tolkien: A Biography* (adapted)

ONE MORE BIOGRAPHICAL TIDBIT

Question: What were Tolkien's worst battlefield memories in World War I?

Answer: During World War I, in France, Tolkien and his fellow British soldiers slept in a dugout filled with lice. A medical officer gave them some ointment he said was guaranteed to keep the lice from biting the soldiers. In his own words, Tolkien recalls what happened: "We anointed ourselves all over with the stuff and again lay down in great hopes, but it was not to be, because instead of discouraging them it seemed to act like a kind of **hors d'oeuvre** [*appetizer*] and the little beggars went at their feast with renewed **vigor** [*energy*]."

All we have to decide is what to do
with the time that is given us.

—J. R. R. Tolkien, *The Fellowship of the Ring*

DR. SEUSS: SILLY BUT GREAT RHYMES AND DRAWINGS

Theodor Seuss Geisel wrote sixteen of the top 100 children's books of all time, selling over 200 million copies. He was the author famous for writing many books with silly but unforgettable rhymes like "I am Sam. Sam-I-am. Do you like green eggs and ham?"

In 1985, Princeton University awarded honorary degrees to six people. An honorary degree is awarded to someone who has done something important for the world. The students were most excited about one of the people being honored. When a tall, thin man with a gray beard stood up, they all leaped to their feet. "I am Sam," they chanted. "Sam-I-am." Then they recited from memory all of Green Eggs and Ham. *It was a special way to show Theodor Geisel, better known as Dr. Seuss, how much his books meant to them.*

—Janet Pascal, *Who Was Dr. Seuss?*

TWIN PARAGRAPHS

A twin paragraph is a paragraph built the same way as a model paragraph. In other words, a twin paragraph is an imitation of the way the sentences in a model paragraph are built.

Following are three activities where you build a twin paragraph for the model paragraph. Although the paragraphs are all built alike, the content is different. Each paragraph is about a different tidbit from Dr. Seuss' biography.

MODEL PARAGRAPH

(1) When Ted was young and had trouble sleeping at night, his mother would calm him down with some rhymes she created to help sell the pies. (2) From listening to his mother reciting those rhymes at that young age, Ted became familiar with language and rhyming words. (3) Although he was a little boy, this experience became a **prime** [*big*] influence on him when he became known as Dr. Seuss.

—Sam Rodgers, *The Life of Dr. Seuss* (adapted)

ACTIVITY 1: MATCHING SENTENCE PARTS

Match the sentence parts from the scrambled imitation sentence to the same sentence parts from the model sentence. When you finish, write out the twin paragraph, focusing on how the equivalent sentence parts are built alike.

Model Sentence	Scrambled Imitation Sentence
Sentence One	
1. When Ted was young	a. and had begun working on books
2. and had trouble sleeping at night,	b. to carry along the plot
3. his mother would calm him down with some rhymes	c. when Seuss was married
	d. his illustrations would tell his story with vivid characters
4. she created	
5. to help sell the pies.	e. he created
Sentence Two	
6. From listening to his mother	f. in very catchy rhymes
7. reciting those rhymes	g. from working on the characters
8. at that young age,	h. with the Grinch and Sam-I-am
9. Ted became familiar	i. Seuss became famous
10. with language and rhyming words.	j. telling his stories

Sentence Three	
11. Although he was a little boy,	**k.** when his popularity grew as an author
12. this experience	**l.** because he was a unique storyteller
13. became a prime influence on him	**m.** his writing
14. when he became known as Dr. Seuss.	**n.** was his main occupation in life

ACTIVITY 2: UNSCRAMBLING TO IMITATE

Build an imitation of the model paragraph by unscrambling the sentence parts. When you finish, write out the twin paragraph, focusing on how the equivalent sentence parts are built alike.

On the Mark: Use a comma where it appears in the model.

> ***Model Sentence One:*** When Ted was young and had trouble sleeping at night, his mother would calm him down with some rhymes she created to help sell the pies.

1a. with a request the editor made

1b. to help build children's interest

1c. and had problems teaching with boring books

1d. his publisher did challenge Dr. Seuss then

1e. after teachers became concerned

> ***Model Sentence Two:*** From listening to his mother reciting those rhymes at that young age, Ted became familiar with language and rhyming words.

2a. for beginning readers

2b. after learning of his publisher

2c. limiting the book's words to 250

2d. Dr. Seuss succeeded with rhyme and readability

Model Sentence Three: Although he was a little boy, this experience became a prime influence on him when he became known as Dr. Seuss.

3a. was an unboring book for children

3b. his book

3c. after they became entertained by its rhymes

3d. although it used only 236 words

ACTIVITY 3: COMBINING TO IMITATE

Combine bolded sentence parts to build an imitation of the model sentence. When you finish, write out the twin paragraph, focusing on how the equivalent sentence parts are built alike.

On the Mark: Use a comma where it appears in the model.

Model Sentence One: When Ted was young and had trouble sleeping at night, his mother would calm him down with some rhymes she created to help sell the pies.

1a. When Dr. Seuss was an illustrator, a change happened.

1b. Seuss changed **and had ideas drawing his animals**.

1c. The change was **he drew his whales**.

1d. With long eyelashes he drew the whales.

1e. The eyelashes **he enlarged**.

1f. He did the silly whale drawings **to make them more memorable**.

Model Sentence Two: From listening to his mother reciting those rhymes at that young age, Ted became familiar with language and rhyming words.

2a. **From looking at his characters telling their stories** Dr. Seuss began something.

2b. He studied his characters **in such silly illustrations**.

2c. It was then that **Dr. Seuss started experimenting**.

2d. His experimental drawings were **with droopy faces and funny buildings**.

Model Sentence Three: Although he was a little boy, this experience became a prime influence on him when he became known as Dr. Seuss.

3a. His rhymes were great **although illustrations were an important part**.

3b. The main outcome was that **his trademark became a silly verse**.

3c. The verse was **in rhyme**.

3d. That rhyming trademark always was used **when his popularity grew**.

3e. The stories were written **as an author**.

YOUR TURN: NONFICTION PARAGRAPH IMITATION

Now that you have produced three imitations of the same model paragraph, write your own imitation of that model paragraph. After learning more online or offline about a nonfiction topic, tell information your readers might not know about any of these topics: *animals, culture, entertainment, health, history, inventions, media, pets, politics, religion, science, space, sports, technology, transportation,* or write a paragraph with a new biographical tidbit about Dr. Seuss.

MODEL PARAGRAPH

(1) When Ted was young and had trouble sleeping at night, his mother would calm him down with some rhymes she created to help sell the pies. (2) From listening to his mother reciting those rhymes at that young age, Ted became familiar with language and rhyming words. (3) Although he was a little boy, this experience became a prime influence on him when he became known as Dr. Seuss.

—Sam Rodgers, *The Life of Dr. Seuss* (adapted)

ONE MORE BIOGRAPHICAL TIDBIT

Question: Why was Dr. Seuss called a doctor when he wasn't a doctor?

Answer: He put Dr. as part of his author's name because his dad had always hoped he'd become a doctor, but he never did. He was, though, another kind of doctor. Princeton University awarded him an honorary academic doctorate.

THE BIG DEAL: WRITING A BIOGRAPHICAL ESSAY

Congratulations on imitating well-built paragraphs about each of those popular authors in the last section. Now, put those skills to work on a longer piece of your own nonfiction writing about another popular author.

WRITING PROCESS

Researching: Find online or offline some interesting biographical tidbits about a popular author to describe in an essay three to five paragraphs long. Some possibilities include these authors, or choose some other popular author you like.

- Louisa May Alcott, *Little Women*
- J. M. (James Matthew) Barrie, *Peter Pan*
- L. Frank Baum, *The Wizard of Oz*
- Edgar Rice Burroughs, *Tarzan*
- Lewis Carroll, *Alice in Wonderland*
- Roald Dahl, *Willie Wonka and the Chocolate Factory*
- Kate DiCamillo, *The Tale of Despereaux*
- Norton Juster, *The Phantom Tollbooth*
- Madeleine L'Engle, *A Wrinkle in Time*
- C. S. (Clive Staples) Lewis, *The Chronicles of Narnia*
- Lucy M. Montgomery, *Anne of Green Gables*
- Beatrix Potter, *The Tale of Peter Rabbit*
- Maurice Sendak, *Where the Wild Things Are*
- Lemony Snicket, *A Series of Unfortunate Events*

- Jules Verne, *Twenty Thousand Leagues Under the Sea*
- Margery Williams, *The Velveteen Rabbit*

Prewriting: From your research, list facts and details about the biographical tidbit for your author.

Drafting: Draft an essay of three to five paragraphs with information about your popular author.

Imitating: For *one* of your essay's paragraphs, imitate any one of the five paragraph models that follow. Build your sentences like those of the model but write about your author. You are already familiar with all five model paragraphs because you practiced and imitated how their sentences are built. For the rest of your paragraphs, without imitating any models, build your sentences equally effectively.

J. K. ROWLING

(1) When she sat down with pen and paper and began to write about the adventures of Harry Potter, a smile crossed her face. (2) Her expressive eyes, framed by long wavy hair, grew even wider. (3) Her pen slashed across the paper like a lightning bolt. (4) In her mind, a door to a delightful new world of imagination and wonder opened wide, and she was about to enter.

A. A. MILNE

(1) At the age of two, young Alan began to read, pleasing his father, while his older brothers struggled to do the same. (2) Alan could write before he was five years old and entered kindergarten. (3) Every morning, Ken and his governess, Beatrice Edwards, walked Alan to school, where he continued to develop his reading and writing skills at a remarkable pace, foreshadowing his literary career.

E. B. WHITE

(1) While he was sick in bed, a fearless young house mouse visited the child Elwyn in his bedroom and was interested enough in this large but quiet neighbor to gradually become a tamed pet. (2) Elwyn supplied the mouse with a little house and watched closely as the mouse explored with its tiny paws and turned its dark eyes to look up at the boy. (3) He even taught it several tricks.

J. R. R. TOLKIEN

(1) When Ronald was beginning to walk, he stumbled on a tarantula. (2) It bit him, and he ran in terror until the nurse snatched him up and sucked out the poison. (3) When he grew up, he could remember running in fear through long, dead grass. (4) In his stories, Tolkien wrote more than once of monstrous spiders with venomous bites.

DR. SEUSS

(1) When Ted was young and had trouble sleeping at night, his mother would calm him down with some rhymes she created to help sell the pies. (2) From listening to his mother reciting those rhymes at that young age, Ted became familiar with language and rhyming words. (3) Although he was a little boy, this experience became a prime influence on him when he became known as Dr. Seuss.

Peer responding: Exchange your draft with other students in your class for oral or written suggestions to improve your paragraph. Give them suggestions, too, about their drafts. Using suggestions from your peers, revise until your paragraph is finished.

Creating a Title: Create a memorable title and subtitle, with a colon between them. *Example:* "J. M. Barrie: The Author Who Never Grew Up."

Good children's literature appeals not only to the child in the adult, but to the adult in the child.

—Johann Wolfgang von Goethe

WORDS OF WIT AND WISDOM

These memorable quotations are from stories by beloved popular authors. Perhaps you'll enjoy some so much you'll read the books from which they come, as have millions of readers who cherish their books.

1. Happiness can be found even in the darkest of times, if one only remembers to turn on the light.

   —J. K. Rowling, *Harry Potter and the Prisoner of Azkaban*

2. You must never feel badly about making mistakes . . . as long as you take the trouble to learn from them. For you often learn more by being wrong for the right reasons than you do by being right for the wrong reasons.

   —Norton Juster, *The Phantom Tollbooth*

3. I don't understand it any more than you do, but one thing I've learned is that you don't have to understand things for them to be.

   —Madeleine L'Engle, *A Wrinkle in Time*

4. "What day is it?" asked Winnie the Pooh. "It's today," squeaked Piglet. "My favorite day," said Pooh.

   —A. A. Milne, *The Adventures of Winnie the Pooh*

5. Sometimes I've believed as many as six impossible things before breakfast.

   —Lewis Carroll, *Through the Looking Glass*

6. You're mad, bonkers, completely off your head. But I'll tell you a secret. All the best people are.

   —Lewis Carroll, *Alice in Wonderland*

7. When someone is crying, of course, the noble thing to do is to comfort them. But if someone is trying to hide their tears, it may also be noble to pretend you do not notice them.

    —Lemony Snicket, *A Series of Unfortunate Events*

8. The moment you doubt that you can fly you cease forever to be able to do it.

    —J. M. (James Matthew) Barrie, *Peter Pan*

9. So many things are possible just as long as you don't know they're impossible.

    —Norton Juster, *The Phantom Tollbooth*

10. Of course it's happening inside your head, Harry, but why on earth should that mean that it is not real?

    —J. K. Rowling, *Harry Potter and the Deathly Hallows*

11. By the time you are Real, most of your hair has been loved off, and your eyes drop out and you get loose in the joints and very shabby. But these things don't matter at all, because once you are Real you can't be ugly, except to people who don't understand.

    —Margery Williams, *The Velveteen Rabbit*

12. I am not afraid of storms for I am learning how to sail my ship.

    —Louisa May Alcott, *Little Women*

13. There is nothing sweeter in this sad world than the sound of someone you love calling your name.

    —Kate DiCamillo, *The Tale of Despereaux*

14. How lucky I am to have something that makes saying goodbye so hard.

    —A. A. Milne, *The Adventures of Winnie the Pooh*

15. A person who has good thoughts cannot ever be ugly. You can have a wonky nose and a crooked chin and stick out teeth, but if you have good thoughts they will shine out of your face like sunbeams and you will always look lovely.

—Roald Dahl, *The Twits*

16. Tomorrow is always fresh, with no mistakes in it.

—Lucy M. Montgomery, *Anne of Green Gables*

****

BECOMING A WRITER

The quotation that follows is the ending of E. B. White's *Charlotte's Web*, a beloved heartwarming but also heartbreaking story of the friendship between a pig named Wilbur, who can talk, and a spider named Charlotte, who can write:

It is not often that someone comes along who is a true friend and a good writer. Charlotte was both.

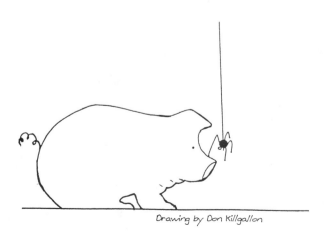

Drawing by Don Killgallon

We hope that you have already learned to be a true friend, and that Nonfiction for Elementary School: A Sentence-Composing Approach *has helped you learn to become a better writer. We, the coauthors, send you our best wishes for success in writing and in friendship.*

—Don and Jenny Killgallon